A FUNCTIONAL APPROACH
TO RELIGIOUS EDUCATION

A FUNCTIONAL APPROACH
TO RELIGIOUS EDUCATION

By

ERNEST J. CHAVE

THE UNIVERSITY OF CHICAGO PRESS
CHICAGO · ILLINOIS

THE UNIVERSITY OF CHICAGO PRESS, CHICAGO 37
Cambridge University Press, London, N.W. 1, England
W. J. Gage & Co., Limited, Toronto 2B, Canada

Introduction

THIS book sets forth a functional analysis of religion and a program of religious education based upon that point of view. Its basic assumption is that religion arises in the primary adjustments of life and is pervasive of all life. While religion is frequently identified with certain theological ideas and group mores, its fundamental characteristics lie much deeper in the organizing and evaluating experiences of daily living. These experiences are describable at all age levels, in the varied relationships of life, and are subject to educational development. The particular analysis given herein grew into form over a period of years, and has been used with persons of different faiths and cultural backgrounds, its terminology proving meaningful and usable for the purposes designated.

The author recognizes two great handicaps to the effective functioning of religion in the modern world—sectarianism and supernaturalism—and seeks to show that these two historical developments are not essentials in the inherent nature of religion and are foreign to its free operation in a modern world. In so doing, he indicts any attempt to classify this functional approach as either humanistic or theistic; for these terms are too vague to make a meaningful dilemma. The functional approach emphasizes the responsibility of man for a large share in his own salvation, but it acknowledges the creative personality-producing forces which give man birth and capacity to function as an intelligent, discriminating, self-conscious being. Sectarian institutions exhaust their strength and dissipate their influence in endless discussions of theological issues. They maintain their differences by systems of indoctrination instead of permitting free inquiry into assumptions and practices. Supernaturalism is a prescientific view of the world, and though many try to rationalize it in order to make it fit a modern world, it leaves a blurred theistic symbolism. A naturalistic and functional approach, on the other hand, offers a basis for a more stable and inspiring faith, with a comprehensive and integrated view of reality. It enables one to be more exact in reference to the processes of the universe than is usual in the common use of theistic terms, and it gives a feeling of confidence that religious faith rests upon experiential data rather than upon presuppositions and labored arguments.

With the naturalistic and functional view of religion the writer joins the educational emphasis on creative experience, in contrast to the ordinary methods of indoctrination. He believes that as long as churches, seminaries, and other agencies of organized religion are primarily concerned to keep alive traditions and look backward for inspiration and direction, they are powerless to deal with modern problems. Religious education must have faith in a developing process, make use of human experience—past and present—and with the creative interaction of free minds move forward to the solution of current issues. It must co-ordinate the latent spiritual forces of society, giving intelligent leadership and working in close co-operation with social, economic, and political movements on a world-wide scale. It must present a comprehensive program for transforming personal-social life by the united efforts of spiritually sensitized parents, teachers, and leaders in every realm of life.

The writer is indebted to the many who have co-operated with him as he has made this study over an extended period of nearly ten years. The functional analysis was developed gradually in class discussions, in conferences on personality measurement, and in frequent conversations with colleagues and other religious educators. It was first presented to the Quadrennial Assembly of the International Boys' Workers of the Y.M.C.A., in Louisville, in May, 1941. The diagnostic value of this functional analysis was tried out in both public school elementary- and high-school situations and in church and Y.M.C.A. settings. Daily observations were made for six months in school programs, and the principals and staffs of these schools rendered invaluable assistance. Reports of these studies, and the possibilities of a wider community approach in religious education, were discussed in interfaith groups under the auspices of the Religious Education Association.

The development of the Unified Functional Curriculum, described in the Appendix, began in close co-operation with the two ministers of the Hyde Park Baptist Church, Chicago: N. L. Tibbetts and R. W. Schloerb, in whose church the first experimental lessons were used. Two graduate students, Miss Gertrude McIntosh and Mrs. Ross Blake, have aided in gathering and developing materials; and ten churches have used the materials and helped in their revision. The two deans of the Divinity School during the period of this study, E. C. Colwell and B. M. Loomer, have given generous support to the whole project, and the George Davis Bivin Foundation has helped to finance the expenses of the curriculum study. The ideas have grown and taken shape in the stimulating atmosphere of the University of Chicago and in conferences and meetings of many kinds with denominational leaders, workers in the International Council of Religious Education, members of the Religious Education Association, Y.M.C.A. secretarial groups, parent-teacher meetings, and staffs of local churches of different denominations. The manuscript has been read critically by Mrs. S. L. Fahs, Miss Edna Acheson, H. N. Wieman, B. M. Loomer, and others; and a number of their suggestions have been incorporated in the final form of this writing.

The concepts, techniques, and programs of the book are the result of years of working on practical problems. The aim of the book is constructive at every point, and wherever there is an indictment of traditional ideas or methods, there is an attempt to present the most promising lines of modern thought and practice. Ideas have been borrowed freely from progressive writers in both general and religious education. The view is dynamic, with faith in the "divine" laws of personal-social growth. (The word "divine" is used throughout this book to indicate the essential nature of the growth process evident in the spiritual realization of latent human possibilities.)

What is presented herein is but a beginning of what the writer hopes may be a radical revision of concepts, ritual, materials, and programs of religious education. Much has been done, and this book is but a small contribution in a movement that is steadily growing. The educational programs for the reconstruction of the world need to be deeply spiritualized, and religious education must visualize the gigantic task and give leadership that transcends sectarianism and that integrates constructive forces wherever they may be found. The leavening forces of religion are at work in all types of organizations, its varied functional forms needing to be identified and unified. While theologians and philosophers struggle for adequate metaphysics for an expanding universe, let educators move forward with working functional concepts and values to help organize personal-social living on a world scale of relationships.

ERNEST J. CHAVE

DIVINITY SCHOOL
UNIVERSITY OF CHICAGO

Contents

Chapter One

Religion Grows in a Changing World

RELIGION is old and ever changing in its concepts and practices. It represents a persistent outreach on the part of man for meanings and values to inspire and to guide him in his restless search for a fuller and a more satisfying life. Throughout the millenniums of history, people have reflected upon their experiences, formulated theories of their universe, and sought ways to attain expanding desires.[1]* They have projected their ideas and ideals into creeds, customs, and institutions and have tried to pass on to oncoming generations their learnings, hopes, and dreams.

The path of progress has not been a broad highway with steady upgrade but has been more like a confusion of jungle trails, now passing through dense undergrowth and swampy lands, again appearing on a high plateau, and occasionally showing on the edge of a high peak. In the course of the centuries the most fantastic ideas and weird practices have stood alongside penetrating insights of philosophers and teachers. Even in the Hebraic-Christian tradition there is a motley collection of strange beliefs and practices, ranging from crude tribal patterns to the ethical and religious messages of the prophets, Jesus, and the apostles. Through the whole history of Christianity there has been a mixture of rational and irrational elements, and even in this scientific age naïve mystical beliefs crowd saner and more comprehensive views.

* Notes and references will be found at the end of the book (p. 162).

1

As the cultures of all nations meet and mingle in this modern age of free intercommunication, it is to be hoped that basic religious ideas and prevailing customs may be subjected to critical examination and fearless reshaping. Instead of sectarian devotees trying to find support for their peculiar ways of thinking and acting, the world needs truth-seeking conferences of humble, openminded scholars representing wide diversities of faith and order. The universe is vast; its processes are complex; knowledge is fragmentary and incomplete; history is being continually revised; and truth must continue to grow. No one can afford to be dogmatic; it is foolish and presumptuous to assume superiority; all need deeper insights, higher values, and more skill in personal-social living. Religious education that would integrate life on its highest levels, correct divisive tendencies, and add a significant quality to general education must keep pace with the deepening creative insights of world thought and gain co-operative action by spiritual leaders in many walks of life.

Religious education cannot look backward for its message, methods, or incentives but must find them in the growing present. Once ox carts served men's needs, and in some parts of the world they do today. But in an age when airplanes crisscross the skies in global encirclements, most people prefer twentieth-century means of travel. Once the witch doctor practiced acceptably with incantations and weird concoctions, and even today some seek like mysterious remedies, but most educated people find greater satisfaction in the services of well-trained physicians and well-equipped hospitals. Once bows and arrows were effective weapons, but today it takes heavily armored tanks, rocket planes, and atomic bombs to make a dent in the lines of an enemy. Once the people of Asia knew nothing of Americans, but now they exchange thought with us daily; and what happens in one country affects the markets and programs of the other. Once religion was chiefly fears and wonderings, mimetic acts and emotional displays, with a few simple beliefs and fixed ceremonies, but today theologians and philosophers struggle to find adequate statements of ideas and ideals. An endless stream of books and periodicals discuss its meanings and practices, and expensive institutions carry on elaborate programs.

Though the ox cart preceded the giant air liner, the latter is only remotely related to the former in principle of operation, construction, or social use. Though the primitive medicine man was the forerunner of the scientifically trained doctor, the latter feels no obligation to follow the former's prescriptions. Here, as elsewhere, it is quite evident that that which functioned satisfactorily in one age may be utterly inadequate for another. Those who sentimentally sing, " 'Tis the old-time religion, and it's good enough for me," and who seek to perpetuate prescientific ideas of revelation, inspiration, salvation, worship, and education, fail to appreciate the values in the cumulative learnings of the centuries. Jesus rebelled against many of the customs and teachings of Hebrew tradition; and, through the years since, religious leaders have repeatedly protested against the bondage of outgrown ideas and customs which have become intrenched in high places. It is reasonable to expect growth in religion as well as in other fields of human experience. In fact, to deny it is to fail to appreciate the fundamental quality of the divine process and the basic character of human learning. Religious education must cease to be the tool of conservatism, indoctrinating immature minds with outgrown ideas and futile customs. It must stimulate creative thought, reconstructing concepts of God, redefining spiritual objectives, and reorganizing religious programs. It must identify the pervasive growth qualities of religion and find ways of making it effective on a world scale in the varied and complex relationships of modern life.

The developing wisdom and idealism of humanity is equal to its problems. This is a day when religion should strengthen high ideals, arouse vision and faith, and call forth leaders to release human possibilities. There are latent in man and in society capacities for much nobler and more satisfying forms of personal-social living than the world has yet seen. There are indications of what man might be in exceptional individuals and groups, and the social sciences are revealing the divine laws of greater achievement. Religion must be conceived in broader terms than the dicta of professional religionists or the sectarian conventionalized patterns of expression. It must be thought of as a divinely implanted growth tendency, or leavening force, such as Jesus repeatedly described in his teachings and parables. The measure of human progress is not in the number of followers of any sect or school of theology but in the degree to which the common life of man has moved upward toward its divine fulfilment. There are many discouraging and depressing facts that challenge faith, but there is always another body of evidence that is encouraging and exhilarating. Following two world wars there is an awful harvest of misery, suffering, crime, and evils of many kinds; and there is still the threat of another more terrible war that may blot out civilization. Millions have to start life anew, gain a philosophy equal to the strains of their hard struggle, and find means for a satisfying living. In America, with more privileges and resources than any other country in the world, there are poverty, economic conflicts, race hatreds, depraved luxury and indulgence, and other evils of many sorts. Yet, on the other hand, there is a United Nations organization, and more concerted effort than ever before in the world's history, to maintain peace and to raise the standards of life for people everywhere. The masses are becoming vocal, finding ways of achieving gains; and agencies with humanitarian ends are multiplying in every land. International, national, and local laws are being made to insure a larger degree of freedom, with better conditions of living, for more people in all countries. Problems are being studied to discover fundamental causes, and educational methods are being used to make people able to help themselves. Intelligent planning is joined to sympathy and prayer. Modern religion needs to be recognized as a world-wide movement, the restless quest of mankind for larger realization of unfulfilled possibilities.

There is no need for a spirit of defeatism in facing the gigantic problems of the postwar world though there is no rational hope for supernatural intervention. In some circles the usual theological solutions of man's troubles, which appear in times of strain and stress, have appeared, and the righteous few, with earnest prayers for divine help have handed over to God the mess that he has permitted. Instead of recognizing the processes of growth, and the only possible way of redemption for responsible persons, such people assume a false role of humility and ask for a miraculous transformation of society. History should have proved to them that this kind of hope is vain, but their cries unto heaven for deliverance are repeated again and again. To many people religion is understood only in supernatural terms, and they constantly magnify mystical experiences and unusual events. They fail to appreciate the much more stable and satisfying qualities of the ordinary processes in which personality is respected and man shares in a growing creative world. They do not recognize the signs of progress and achievement, as man has moved away from caveman struggles for existence, to organized tribal life, to national forms of co-operation, and now into a global pattern of international agreement. They do not see how organized knowledge has relieved man from many of his fears and worries, given him insight into the workings of his universe, and made the possibilities of a rich and ennobling life available for all. The divine processes of growth are marvelous, reaching their maximum in the spiritual maturation of free men and women. Instead of religion degenerating into a futile and shameful conflict over theological doctrines, we should have a working agreement on the discoverable laws of spiritual growth, with world-wide programs of education and social action. One of the main tasks of religious educators would seem to be to identify the growth factors, to clarify the conditions for best spiritual development, and to distribute responsibility for furthering latent possibilities.

Men and women of spiritual purpose and discernment are exerting their influence in business, government, education, recreation, home life, and all the areas of common relationship. Religious education must be conceived as the total comprehensive plan by which leaders in all realms of life co-operate to further the growth of personal-social values and attainments. The formal services of churches and synagogues may continue, and serve important purposes, but they must be thought of as secondary rather than primary factors in the developing spiritual life of humanity. Parents, teachers, labor leaders, management, political leaders, government officials, recreational leaders, radio broadcasters, filmmakers, newspapermen, and the thousands of others who influence public opinion and attitudes, need to be sensitized to spiritual goals and to the interrelated processes by which such may be realized. It is foolish to think that an hour of teaching, or preaching, once a week can transform human nature or release divine powers when the rest of the week is left unconditioned by intelligent spiritual planning. The dualism of sacred and secular must give place to a unified view of the pervasive qualities of religion.

Throughout this book a naturalistic position is assumed rather than a supernaturalistic, on the grounds that naturalism gives religion a much more substantial and realistic basis. As mankind has grown away from fanciful interpretations and personifications of nature toward an objective and systematic study of the phenomena of life, a greater sense of the dynamic stability and resourcefulness of the world order has been developed. It is unfortunate when religion fails to profit by the growing understanding of the processes of the universe, using and trying to rationalize ancient picturizations. In naturalism there is a re-evaluation of the ideas and values of the various systems of religion that the centuries have presented, with a modern statement of the cumulative experience and its meaning for modern faith and action.[2] Instead of trying to make the concepts and interpretations of history, science, and general experience fit some theological pattern, a theology or philosophy of religion is constructed from an integration and evaluation of growing experience. Belief and motivation for living come from a vital, developing appreciation of an inexhaustible creative order in which man is a significant agent rather than from any theory about the creator or sustainer of this order.

Naturalism in no sense ignores the cosmic forces which supernaturalism personifies, nor does it exalt man as a deity, but it seeks to help people adjust their lives most fruitfully to the dependable laws and stimulating privileges of their universe. It does not regard an experience as any more religious because the word God is used to indicate this creative order, but it is free to use the traditional term, or any of its synonyms, when there is clear reference to identifiable and experiential phases of universal processes. Instead of worshiping a blurred image, using formal phrases and ancient imageries of outgrown theologies, a naturalist seeks to find the latent possibilities of life by meditation and reflection upon the growing meanings and values of life. He knows no division of life into sacred and secular; for he has faith in a divine order that encompasses all and that is working for the gradual development of all. He does not exalt extraordinary events as witness of a deity making himself known; for the marvels of the ordinary "natural" world inspire him to share in the co-operative creative process. He may speculate on the ultimate cause and control of his universe, as his supernaturalist friend does, but he rests his faith on reality as he experiences it rather than on a theological assumption or theory about it.

Most religious education is out of focus, giving blurred and confusing pictures of reality. There is little historical appreciation of the ways in which religious ideas and values have grown and no due recognition of the necessarily developmental character of all modern concepts. For instance, the concept of God has a wide range of meanings and is commonly used by people to affirm a dogmatic belief, but it might have a stabilizing and integrating value if it were kept in close reference to growing knowledge of the creative and sustaining forces of the universe which affect man's welfare. Likewise, there is a common practice of reading into the picturesque language of the Bible any meaning that one may feel inspired to use instead of finding therein a fascinating story of changing ideas and practices in changing social conditions of an ancient period in history.

There was a time when spirits and deities were imagined as located in particular places of exceptional experiences, and places of worship were by springs, under particular trees, or in special places revered by traditions. Today many people think of the church as God's house and the special place where he is to be worshiped and experienced. Jesus refused to accept such a limitation on his view of God, though he did rebel against a desecration of the formal center of worship.

The handiwork of the divine is in all creation and his working in all the affairs and processes of life. But the concept of the creator and sustainer of life, the determiner of destiny, must be different today from what it was two thousand or more years ago; for men think today of a universe infinite in space, orderly in its complex operations, with a history that reaches back millions of years and with the earth which is man's home set in the midst of this overwhelming process. The interpretation of man's place in the total scheme of things, the worth of an individual in the multitude who are being born and dying every day, the possibilities of personal-social advancement, and the best methods of achieving optimum growth are not subjects for dogmatic pronouncements or indoctrinating techniques but for keenest critical thought, co-operative search, and continually revised and enriched programs of teaching and action.

It is humbling to realize the fact that only a very small fraction of mankind receive their impressions as to the religious meanings and worth of life from either the liberals or conservatives of the two hundred and fifty sects of the United States. Though the writer once believed that the world was to be saved by the preaching of "the faith once delivered to the saints" and was certain that he had the gospel of salvation, he now knows that there never was a faith once delivered which could be propagated as a magical formula for salvation. He sees Christianity as a minority type of religion, and modernism and fundamentalism as changing interpretation within that body of ideas and practices, while great ethnic faiths reflect other concepts, and the general experience of mankind in an ever interrelated fashion gathers and sorts beliefs and values.

Meanings and goals have been tested and refined in the fires of war, suffering, sorrow, struggle, and privation. They have been critically analyzed, dramatically glorified, poetically embellished, artistically portrayed, oratorically emotionalized, and humbly evaluated by people of every race and country, of varied creeds and loyalties. The ultimate meanings and worth of life have not yet been discovered, but some high peaks have been climbed, and the vistas beyond invite further exploration. Some religious ideas and ideals have been enshrined in sacred scriptures, ceremonies, and institutions; but others are best expressed in the lives of great men and women of the past and present. There may never be one generally accepted theology, philosophy, or system of norms; for man's needs, interests, appreciations, insights, and relationships vary greatly, but there can be a growing mutuality of understanding and respect which will gradually modify all beliefs, practices, and attitudes. A world charter of human rights was drafted by a United Nations conference without benefit of clergy, or with their voice as only a minor influence in the deliberations. Great spiritual ideals are being born and put into action in all realms of life without church sponsorship. The leavening forces of religious ideas and attitudes transcend sects, orthodoxies, and agencies of vested religious interests.

When people recognize the fact that there is nothing fixed or final in theology, beliefs, customs, or institutions, they are free to enlarge their concepts and modify their attitudes and procedures in any phase of religion. It is one thing to appreciate the creative orderly nature of the universe but quite another to posit a personal divine being controlling every part of every process. People need knowledge and imagination before they enter into controversies as to the nature of God. Most theologians and orthodox censors do not do justice to the creator and sustainer of the universe.[3] They do not seem to have conceived of the intricacies in the cosmic order, the marvelous planning, and the multiple possibilities in every process. Think of what is involved in the development of a bulb, as the pattern of growth of the plant, flower, and seed are laid down in it for the reproduction of the species. Consider the mysteries of the genes, the microscopic architects of human growth; and add to these wonders the latent capacities of development and adjustment in a growing personality. Or ask an astronomer to help you ponder the gigantic forces moving celestial bodies through space in orderly and predictable manner. Who, or what, is God? Surely children should not be taught to think of the Spirit, who has moved through the vast realms of time and eternity, and whose handiwork is in such processes as we have just indicated, as but a kindly man to whom they can chatter. And adults should not grow up thinking, or feeling, in such childish terms.

Likewise, people need to stretch their imagination in thinking of the Word of God. Some limit it to sixty-odd ancient manuscripts whose originals are long lost. They never appreciate the multitude of records which reveal the story of the universe—prehistoric records which scientists help us read, historic interpretations written in the languages of all nations, and contemporary experiences which we study in the light of the past. The Bible gives us a brief account of what a small group of people in a limited area of the earth, in a short period of time, thought of the world processes and the events in which they were participants. It is more of a revelation of these people than of God, but it has been one of the most stimulating records in the history of mankind, causing reflection upon the nature of the world processes and man's place therein.[4] Too many, however, read it in an uncritical, unhistorical way, failing to differentiate between the tribal ideas of a God who demanded appeasement and the later more universal concepts with higher moral attitudes. Many also fail to understand the growth of religious and ethical ideas and ideals in the centuries since the Bible books were written. Religion today is a faith and purpose born out of long experience, and in its highest forms it seeks those conditions which will help everyone to realize fulness of personality in a world order where persons receive primary consideration. Salvation ceases to be a bargaining process between a condemned sinner and a fearful judge who can be satisfied only by a dramatic sacrifice. It becomes a long-time and complex process of growth in which man learns to respect his latent capacities as a discriminating being with responsibility for his choices and actions and finds his deepest satisfactions in using his privileges. It also involves co-operative action and organized effort to correct those conditions which tend to debase and to enslave man, freeing him from such handicaps as poverty, sickness, environmental limitations, ignorance, prejudices, greed, and other evils. In this modern world view, ideologies of religion become commensurate with expanding knowledge; and the changes are reflected in ritual, organization, program, preaching, teaching, and all that is done through religious institutions.

Intrenched forces frequently attempt to block progress, but their resistance is weakened as they are by-passed by advancing united groups of intelligent and enthusiastic workers confident in a larger faith and mission. Individuals may suffer persecution even as Jesus did, but the tides of progress are irresistible. Yet, as we said in beginning, there is no steady march forward; for people are fickle, sometimes eager and expectant, and again fearful and indifferent. When Jesus boldly attacked the evils of his day, setting forth in plain fashion a new gospel of richer and more realistic promise, the common people heard him gladly and the crowds followed him. Yet they were stampeded by the emotional appeals of their old leaders and turned against their redeemer. Only a few disciples understood the critical issues and were ready to pay the cost of change. Today similar conflicts go on between advocates of progressive movements in government, education, economics, social reform, and religion, and the conservative vested interests. When a radical change is proposed, it is branded as socialist, communist, atheist; and prejudices are aroused to confuse the basic issues. Progress is being made, but it is a slow achievement, for there is no miraculous way of saving people. They must learn by experience.

One reason that people seem so hesitant and fearful is that our general educational system fails to develop critical and comprehensive thinking. People are not trained from childhood to examine presuppositions, to analyze generalities, to seek facts, and creatively to develop their experiences. There is too much blind obedience in homes, schools, churches, industry, government, and general life, without persistent questioning and reasoning about matters of belief and conduct. Interests are in the main selfish, narrow, and exclusive. We need a more adventurous spirit that finds satisfaction in explorations, experiments, and complex problems. If we are to have religion which actually leavens society, we must have people who dare to think, who expect change and welcome improvements, who hold many interests in mind, and who can co-operate with one another in effective undertakings. We need bigger personalities, able to live in a unified world and intelligent enough to enjoy co-operative use of the inexhaustible resources of their universe. We need people who are equal to the task of transforming daily living and who do not avoid difficulties by assuming a dualistic philosophy of sacred and secular. This ideal will be realized as general education becomes more critical and comprehensive and as religion loses its defensive sanctity and separateness.

In primitive life, religion emerged out of the common experiences and needs of men and women. It was born out of the desires, frustrations, outreachings, and achievements of daily living, and its hopes, beliefs, and practices permeated all they did. Gradually, original reasons for beliefs and customs disappeared, but many of these ideas and practices persisted and were rationalized on new bases. As cultures intermingled, ideas and forms merged; and religion became increasingly a separate and specialized interest, with an external rather than an internal and pervasive influence. Today we face the critical problem of organized religion struggling to justify its existence while spiritual forces are emerging in all areas of life with religious interpretations independent of ecclesiastical sanctions. The clash is accentuated by the fact that traditional theologies, doctrines, and customs of organized religion are generally expressed in a language and pattern foreign to contemporary thought and use. In America the majority of the population are indifferent to church teachings, and those who do attend some sectarian group seem to show little difference in conduct. The roots of religion are deeper than any system of indoctrination, and the forms of its expression are more vitally related to the attitudes and values of life than are those commonly expressed in formal church relationships. Repeatedly, students, on campuses where theological seminaries and colleges or universities are together, draw contrasts between the spiritual interpretations and emphases in the different institutions.

Yet a change is evident; for organized religion and professional religionists are seeking to integrate and to unify influences working for spiritual enrichment. Theology and philosophy are gaining new vitality as leaders use naturalistic terms and draw their supporting data from varied areas of growing experience. Religious programs are becoming more intimately related to the needs of the common man and to the conditions which limit his full development. Ministers are sharing in outside agencies which work for human welfare and are encouraging their members to do the same. Co-operative enterprises are being launched in which divisive peculiarities are forgotten as larger interests demand thought and united action. Ritual, hymns, teaching materials, and many writings reflect a new concern for modern problems and a faith born out of growing insights and social skills. There is a growing expectation that the ideals expressed in church, or specifically set forth as religious, may have champions in government, business, recreation, and the varied relations of life; and in many cases idealists in the market place seek support from the halls of religion. The possibilities of a pervasive spiritual movement which shall capture the imagination and interests of many people is being voiced by scientists, labor leaders, statesmen, educators, poets, radio commentators, preachers, and other leaders of public thought. These hopes are probably due in large part to the extreme sense of need in a world where basic human values are threatened by disaster. Everything else seems secondary to thinking persons in this critical hour in human history.

As the more pervasive and functional aspects of religion gain ascendancy, the theological, institutional, and historical elements take a secondary place. The latter are recognized as means and not as ends and are evaluated functionally. Thus it is more important to have a good working-view of the universe and its processes than to be familiarly vague in use of the term God. Likewise, it is better to catch the spirit of Jesus in the search for the abundant life than to consume time and energy in controversial discussions about his life or teachings. Whatever one may learn about ancient or modern beliefs; whatever membership one may have in any sect; whatever emotional concern one may have for a religious cause, the critical question is whether one sees clearly, and is committed to, specific ways of religious living. This implies that the characteristics of the spiritual, or religious, can be defined and made explicit by living examples at all age levels. The following chapter makes a functional religious analysis, and the succeeding chapters multiply illustrations of what is included under the various categories of religious experience.

In presenting this functional analysis of religion, the writer over a number of years has found a growing interest and response from both churchmen and those outside. While there are many conservatives and reactionaries who are afraid of any disturbance of traditional beliefs or practices, there is an increasing number of persons, young and old, who are impatient with the limitations and inadequacies of the old. They are eager for change, ready for experimentation, and prepared critically and creatively to support whatever seems promising in a new venture. Through the centuries many individuals and groups have broken away from orthodox systems and released new energies. Jesus stimulated a small group of radicals in the Jewish church, and they launched the Christian movement. Luther and Wesley, in turn, promoted other radical changes and in their day broke the incrustations of religion, setting free its true spirit and power. There are always liberals struggling to maintain conditions that will stimulate free growth of truth and release latent capacities in people. There are always those whose vision, faith, and perseverance are an inspiration to those who seek a better day. In this functional approach we believe we have a practical way of enabling men and women of high purpose and zeal to work together. It is a view of religion which transcends sectarianism, divisive controversy, and rigid tradition. It allows for wide diversity in creative expression, conserves the growing historical appreciations of religion, and provides for direct and indirect attack upon the critical human needs of our day.

In this book we aim, therefore, to do these specific things, as we set forth what we believe are the most promising trends in modern religious education:

1. To make plain what is meant by a functional, dynamic, and naturalistic view of religion, and of religious education, in contrast to the theologically centered and artificially limited set of ideas and practices propagated by indoctrinating methods.

2. To show how a functional approach makes use of the best learnings of both the past and the developing present and how it enlarges and refines the ideas, ideals, and practices of historical religion.

3. To indicate how sectarianism may be transcended, showing how churches and leaders with vision, ready to operate on a functional basis, may play an important role in unifying the spiritual forces of modern society and in elevating standards in all phases of life.

4. To show how responsibility may be distributed in seeking to make religious ideas and ideals operative in a growing fashion, at all age levels, in all areas of the common life, and on a world scale.

5. To present a unified functional curriculum which has been tried

out for several years in varied types of churches, which may be suggestive for the modification and enrichment of existing church-school programs.

6. To suggest how religion may become an integral part of general education, without violating the spirit of the Constitution regarding separation of church and state, when a functional view of religion is used and its primary values and goals are kept clear of sectarian controversies.

7. To encourage religious leaders discontented with existing conditions to co-operate in experimental studies, to seek alliance with like-minded persons, and to find faith in the possibilities of creative development.

Chapter Two

A Functional Analysis of Religion

THERE might be little change if things functioned satisfactorily as first created, but the nature of the world and of man is such that nothing is static. One reason for the difficulty of keeping adolescents in the church is that they do not feel the vitality of growth in the concepts and undertakings of organized religion. They do not feel the challenge of continually adding to their understanding of the basic ideas of religion, of integrating their widening experiences, and of working with others to give adequate expression to growing ideas and ideals. Many artificial means are being used to make religion attractive, but few are ready to subject to thorough critical study the assumptions, language, techniques, and procedures of traditional institutions. Yet the hope of raising the quality of spiritual living and of gaining new respect and interest for religious teachings and practices is in the willingness of people to study it objectively and fearlessly To do this one must analyze it into its constituent factors, giving attention to various aspects of religion as it functions in the growing individual and in society and also as it is known in its historical forms and in its on-going experiential character. Most studies of religion are historical, philosophical, or theological; but in this we take a genetic, valuational, and functional approach. While we recognize the significance of theologies, creeds, rituals, institutions, literature, and many customs as by-products of religion, we look for the living spirit and basic qualities in the primary adjustments of growing

17

persons. We want to be able to identify the kinds of experiences in which children, youth, and adults may find the religious meanings and values of life. We assume that religion is pervasive of all life and that it can be found functioning at all age levels as a reflective, valuational, and creative process.

Two analogies may help to indicate what is being attempted in this functional analysis of religion.[1] The first is seen in the ways that a plant such as a chrysanthemum might be studied. A scientist might gather specimens of different varieties; investigate the history of the plant; note similarities and differences in species; make a chemical analysis of various parts; examine cell structures; study the function of various parts, forms, colorings, and constituents; experiment with conditions of soil, moisture, temperature, and light; and gradually gather a mass of data relative to the nature and growth of chrysanthemums. An array of dissected parts, statistical facts, and well-arranged information from such a study would not look much like a chrysanthemum, but one who made a study of this kind would have a basis for appreciation different from that of a casual observer. This type of analysis is not the only kind that can be made; for there are other values which a scientist does not always experience. If he were an invalid, suffering greatly and unable to move, a bouquet of chrysanthemums brought by a friend would have new meanings which he might not have considered in his laboratory. He might remember a day when he presented a big "mum" to a girl whom he took for the first time to a football game, and other meanings and treasured values would arise. Objects and experiences have many possible meanings depending upon the functions they serve in people's interests and needs.

Another illustration of what an analysis may do to help us describe a set of experiences may be taken from the field of mental measurement. With only a superficial acquaintance, we differentiate people into classes as dull, bright, inferior, superior, ordinary, or some such general category. But we might give them intelligence tests, graded series of questions and problems, by which they could be rated on a scale and each given an Intelligence Quotient. Or we could use more recent diagnostic instruments, getting a factorial analysis and finding not only the degree but also the type of intelligence. By a further study of educational achievement, behavior in varied situations, and comparison with judgments of others, one could have a fairly good basis for estimating how anyone on whom one could get data of this kind would function in typical situations. Religion is another complex body of experiences on which it is desirable to get analytic data, especially as one is concerned with developing an educational program to further its best functioning in individuals and in society, under widely varying conditions.

In all areas of education there is a growing tendency to give more attention to functional analyses and methods of such studies than to testing accumulation of knowledge as a mark of culture and learning.[2] In biology the major interest is in the function of organs and arrangement of parts rather than upon structure, the latter being incidental in the former kind of learning. In geography attention is centered upon the value of mountains, rivers, soils, climate, and other factors which serve the needs of man, with listings, mappings, and other descriptions secondary. In sociology the history of organizations and present structure of society are studied from the standpoint of how they have functioned, or are functioning, for the welfare of people. Even in subjects such as art there is a growing appreciation of the function of color, design, texture, arrangement, and the like in depicting meanings and in giving desired impressions; and while appreciation of wholes is still important, wholes take on different values as the significance of parts is understood.

So, also, in religion there is an increasing interest in the functional aspects of concepts, doctrines, institutions, and practices. Theology is recognized as a constantly creative attempt to adjust ideas to changing experiences. Ethical teachings, cult requirements, and the changing use of symbols, ceremonies, and traditions, reflect the practical needs and interests of the times. History reveals the functional qualities of different forms, interpretations, and stresses in different cultures and conditions, showing wide divergencies in points of view. One especially interesting factor in this process has been the way in which supernatural ideas, legends, and mysteries have been used to keep the masses in control. Long after leaders lose their faith in literal beliefs of this kind they keep the common people in conformity to established customs. Even today liberals frequently justify the use of outgrown forms as necessary to meet the expectations of the uncritical masses. They recognize the difficulties involved in making radical changes. Yet, after occupation of Japan, there was little hesitancy in shattering the faith of millions in Shintoism, the conquerors having assumed that this legendary religion could be replaced by a more intelligent and democratic system of thought. Judaism and Christianity might ponder the ancient teaching, "Thou hypocrite, cast out first the beam out of thine own eye; and then shalt thou see clearly to cast out the mote out of thy brother's eye."

The primary considerations in the choice and use of the ten types of religious experience described hereunder, and assumed to be a fairly comprehensive factorial analysis from a functional point of view, have been the following: (1) interest in the developmental nature of religion, with special concern for the formative period of childhood and youth; (2) recognition of the futility of trying to condition fundamental ideas, attitudes, and habits by merely using the brief periods of the ordinary church program; (3) sense of the pervasive qualities of religion, with increasing appreciation of the constructive spiritual influences of better homes, schools, and other agencies of our modern society;[3] (4) recognition of the need for a language of common discourse which might aid in identifying the primary elements of religious experience and in enabling people in different agencies to co-operate more effectively; (5) response which has been given to the presentation of these ideas and analytic categories by people of widely differing religious background and by those engaged in widely different social tasks; (6) gradual growth and enrichment of this analysis over a period of more than ten years, with increasing meaning and widening use; and (7) appraisal of what is being done in the average as well as in the best churches, with an urgent sense of need for radical changes in point of view, methods, and materials in religious education.

The ten categories are convenient classifications that have proved meaningful to a wide range of persons, culturally, religiously, and socially differentiated. While neither the number ten nor the names given to the categories are final, they have served to identify elements which may be found at any age level, in varied life situations, and in the behavior of both naturalists and supernaturalists, and in those who call themselves agnostics and atheists. This analysis recognizes differences in both kind and degree of spirituality and shows why those differences occur. The order of listing in our ten-point analysis is somewhat arbitrary; for the categories are not exclusive. Elements in each tend to overlap; for they are inseparable parts of a living whole. What we hope to do is to focus attention on different factors, trusting that following a careful analysis the re-synthesized meanings will be more enlightening. Since religion is so complex, and human experiences constantly changing, it is inevitable that interpretations of different persons will differ in classification of a situation or response. In studying religious behavior, using this factorial analysis, one must keep in mind interrelated experiences; for any particular factor is significant only as it contributes to a balanced developing whole.

Our general assumption is that wherever and whenever these kinds of experiences are being developed spiritual goals are being realized, whether they take place in church, home, school, playground, business, or other relationship. Religious growth is relevant in all these categories, the influence of church or other agency being evaluated with reference to the opportunities they afford for satisfying experiences along these lines. The analysis attempts to present a comprehensive basis for outlining objectives for setting up programs of religious education and for evaluating the effectiveness of a program or agency in helping to make religion function in daily life. To the degree that this analysis fails to be comprehensive there is need for its modification by change of categories or by inclusion of types of experience that are not herein listed or suggested. The categories are not traits but constellations of experiences subsumed under convenient headings and are supposed to include all kinds in the maturing situations from infancy to adulthood. They are intended to describe religion as it operates in growing lives. We list the ten categories and then expand their meanings to indicate the ways in which these varied experiences may be expected to be found.

1. Sense of worth
2. Social sensitivity
3. Appreciation of the universe
4. Discrimination in values
5. Responsibility and accountability
6. Co-operative fellowship
7. Quest for truth and realization of values
8. Integration of experiences into a working philosophy of life
9. Appreciation of historical continuity
10. Participation in group celebrations

1. *Sense of worth.*—One becomes religious to the degree that one arises above the animal and mechanistic levels of reaction and functions as an intelligent person, making discriminating choices, setting goals, and working toward chosen ends. One must see widening possibilities, feel significant as a member of society, and find satisfaction in being a creative member of the universe. One must feel motivation toward fulness of life. Wherever and whenever anyone is helped to gain self-respect, to feel latent worth, and to work for ends that further personal-social values, the objectives of religion are being achieved. This sense of worth begins in the normal egocentric tendencies of every child, matures spiritually as the self becomes identified

with others, and deepens with growing social interests. It is furthered as individual differences are respected, special talents are given opportunities for expression, and freedom for initiative is encouraged. It is stimulated by examples of lives which rise above the average, by sympathetic understanding and recognition, and by successes in overcoming handicaps and difficult problems.

In the Christian religion it has been customary to speak of man as a son of God, made in his image, and with peculiar rights as one maintains loyalty to his commands. Various theological doctrines have been propounded to preserve this relationship when sin has caused man to lose his birthright, but man's status has always been in jeopardy in certain theological schools. The naturalistic position does not need to labor to give or to maintain worth in the cosmic scheme, for it takes what it finds and studies the laws of growth. Man is the one type of self-conscious being, able to co-operate in a developmental process, able to function appreciatively in a world order of complex relationships; and he seems to give meaning and worth to the whole scheme. Naturalism does not introduce theories about a deity to lessen appreciation of man's natural worth and possibilities of growth but presses forward to realize the fulness of possibilities of a real world. This functional approach lifts out the many encouraging evidences of privileges and faces frankly the discouraging and frustrating facts of the upward climb. Religion has too often set forth ideals without considering how those ideals could be attained for the majority of people. When religious forces are recognized as permeating education, government, economic planning, recreation, and all forms of social expression, the true worth of man will have been acknowledged, and the lines of progress will have been demonstrated.[4] The ideal figure of Christianity had a high sense of worth and lived a life of worth to society, leaving an example of how the ordinary life may be transformed into one of supreme worthfulness.

2. *Social sensitivity.*—A necessary correlative to a healthy sense of worth is a desire to help others realize their potentialities. It involves

the ability to take the role of others, to put the Golden Rule into action. It is the essence of Christian love, the proof of brotherliness, transcending differences of race, class, nationality, creed, age, or disposition. It means the control of one's own desires in order to give room for the fulfilment of the needs and desires of others. It is a measure of a personality big enough to be religious. While it is not easy in our complex society to be just or practical in generosity, we can treat all others as ends rather than as means to our selfish advancement. It is difficult to be socially sensitive in a world where injustice, greed, prejudice, hate, fear, and other unsocial attitudes and acts are met at every turn. It is especially hard for children to develop kindly attitudes when they live in homes or communities where the struggle for existence is keen and where human qualities are at a low level. Careful study of many specific situations is needed to know how to love with wisdom, to serve others without destroying their self-respect, and to be able to see faults and yet to work sympathetically in spite of them. It is more common to exalt the abstract virtues of love and brotherliness than to give evidence of their practicality. God is frequently called the spirit of love, the father of all men, concerned with the needs of every individual, but the dogma is stated without proof of the universality of this good spirit. Nevertheless, this quality of life is the condition for the most beautiful and satisfying human attainments; and its opposite means hate, war, conflict, and endless suffering. Social sensitivity has countless forms—parental love, loyalty of friends, individual and organized charity, a doctor's service to the needy, patient helpfulness of a teacher toward a pupil, thoughtfulness of an employer for an employee, kindliness of a soldier for a wounded enemy, unpatronizing respect of a child by an adult, tactful help given to a depressed unfortunate, and all the ordinary courtesies which make life more cheerful and worth while. Social sensitivity is probably the primary test and ultimate goal of spirituality: "Thou shalt love thy neighbor as thyself."

3. *Appreciation of the universe.*—In religion, people think of the

cosmic setting of life and seek universal principles to stabilize thought and action. They feel that the processes of the world are not blind forces without respect for human values but that man has a significant place as a co-worker in a developing program that has multiple possibilities. They seek to understand the nature and purpose of the creative, personality-producing power which gives us birth and stimulates us to fulfil our capacities. From a functional point of view a growing appreciation of the processes is more important than theological speculations about God; for any study of religious history shows that God is always a reflection of world views. In science, man studies observable phenomena, systematically organizes his facts, builds theories as to the underlying processes, and then seeks to test his theories by observation and experimentation. In religion, man evaluates these learnings for human welfare, seeking as far as possible to get a philosophy of underlying meanings that will give incentive to fullest personal-social living. A reverent appreciation of the universe may be expressed in hymns of praise or in enjoyment of natural beauty and unselfish use of natural resources. It may lead some to assume a personal God as the creative power behind all, while others may use the historical term as a symbol for certain integrative and creative phases of the world processes, and still others may prefer to deal directly with reality as they find it without personifying it or without hypothecating any particular kind of God. In worship one may direct thought and words to the God he pictures immanent or transcendant; or he may bow in thankful appreciation for the resources and privileges of an inexhaustible world and meditate upon its meaning for himself and his fellow-men. From a functional point of view one may be religious without assuming a theistic view, and, if one does assume a God, one must relate the concept to the facts of critical experience; for the end-point is fruitful spiritual adjustment to reality, an enhancement of personal-social values because of faith in the resources and processes of the world in which we live, move, and have our being.

4. *Discrimination in values.*—Spiritual living requires intelligent differentiation between the alternatives which life offers, with a readiness to sacrifice lesser values for the sake of achieving greater. One proves capacity to transcend chance likes and dislikes, to organize purposes and actions about chosen values and goals, to work with persistent effort to achieve them. To the degree that one senses the alternatives in given situations, feels the differences between values, and makes wise choices, one is religious. To the degree that one gains incentive to live above the average, that one stops making excuses for shortcomings and gets satisfaction out of superior qualities of objects and events, one is religious. Whatever experiences help to refine tastes and manner of life, to widen the gap between blind impulses and intelligent choice, and to stimulate interest in the upward climb, are contributing toward religious growth. Theology has constructed elaborate theories about the idea of sacrifice, and for some people the word implies the special act of sacrifice by Jesus to meet the judicial requirements of his father God. Without discussion of this legalistic view of religion let us ask how far the spirit of sacrifice is considered an essential quality of the religious life. Many will wear a cross and give lip service to doctrines of the Atonement without feeling the obligation to sacrifice lesser values for greater, without even perceiving what are the enduring and ennobling values of life. The little child must learn to appreciate the values of discrimination and sacrifice, and, as one grows, the tests of choice and sacrifice penetrate every thought and act. They are fundamental conditions of spiritual progress.

5. *Responsibility and accountability.*—Religion affirms that no one can be a law unto himself, that each man's freedom is bounded by the next man's like need for similar freedom. Freedom is a condition for fulfilment of highest values, but it implies responsibility and accountability. One must recognize one's obligations to one's family, neighborhood, church, school, government, cosmic order, to all persons and groups with whom one is related in the co-operative business

of living. Religion involves all that is included under such terms as "duty," "conscience," "dependability," "sense of guilt for unsocial conduct," "appreciation of freedom," "accepting one's share in social living." If man had been made an automaton, all responsibility for his functioning would have rested upon the Cosmic Mechanician, but since man has capacity to learn by experience and has intelligence to choose and to act, he must accept responsibility for his own acts and for those in which he has a co-operative share.

One begins life in a home which is set in an organized community, which is a part of a richly endowed universe; and, hence, it is foolish for anyone to assert independence or selfish interests. One must learn to respect those with whom one is inseparably related; for good living is a two-way, mutual process. If parents expect co-operation, they must show respect for children's rights and give them trust and responsibility. If communities want democratic, responsible citizens, law must not seem arbitrary but for the good of all. If religion is to be thought of as more than the arbitrary demands of an almighty power, people must feel that the principles of daily living allow for freedom and responsibility. Intelligent democratic living requires joint accountability to one's best self and to others. An educational plan for developing responsibility must be realistic, carefully graduated to the abilities and resources of both young and old. Religious exhortations must be joined to practical suggestions for implementation. It is not good religion to pray, "Lord, teach us how," or, "God, give us wisdom," when the need is to use the knowledge we have or that we are able to get. Religious living rightly expects more of privileged people than of those who lack economic goods, friends, culture, health, or other resource at a decent twentieth-century level. Jesus' Parable of the Talents is still a good illustration of what responsible living means.

6. *Co-operative fellowship.*—As the first category dealt with the individual, so this deals with the essential qualities of transformed group life. The ideals of the kingdom of God are but the vision of a social order in which each and all have the best conditions possible for

realization of their several possibilities because of the co-operative fellowship which binds person to person with common interests and goals. Just as individuals must seek to understand their worth and have ambitions to achieve their best, so, also, must groups. Everyone needs to feel identification with a respectable family and community, with organizations and movements doing significant things for public welfare, with agencies which give wholesome outlet to one's abilities and desires. It is the task of religious education to stimulate people to participate critically and creatively in various forms of group life, so that they do not feel themselves helpless victims of established conditions but have satisfaction in helping to keep the groups to which they belong interesting and effective. A church should provide congenial and energizing fellowship around projects affecting human values and ideas, but co-operative fellowship is just as religious if it occurs at a high level in any other group situation. In fact, the church should give perspective, stimulation, and suggestive guidance for the finest forms of group activities in schools, clubs, business, labor unions, homes, and all kinds of organizations of children, youth, and adults. When religious education reaches out to promote critical study of needs, plans, and outcomes in current organizations, giving motivation toward unselfish co-operative service in the many areas of local, national, and international relationship, religion will come into its fulness of power. Jesus' parables of the kingdom of God have many suggestions as to how this spirit of fellowship may be expected gradually to transform society.

7. *Quest for truth and realization of values.*—Religion is a persistent quest, with growing insight for the basic meanings and values of life, and a consequent sustained effort to extend spiritual learnings and to realize human possibilities. It is a due respect for the complexities of life and for the necessarily slow process of achieving ideals. It maintains a critical attitude toward all dogmatic simplifications of truth and toward all attempts to reach significant gains by irrational means. It is a dynamic faith which resists apologetic and defeatist attitudes

and finds a real joy in doing hard things. Truth is a growing appreciation of reality and not an authoritarian opinion or a sacred tradition. The difference between facts and interpretations of facts, and between certainty and hypothesis, needs to be carefully studied; for most theological statements about God, prayer, right and wrong, salvation, the Bible, the church, and other like concepts are not verifiable truths. If they were, we would not have so many divergent statements and bitter controversies. The spiritual quest is a natural outgrowth of native curiosity, grows with widening experience, and is kept alive by the inability to get final answers to life's most interesting and significant problems. Whenever religion becomes static in its creeds and customs, it tends to be defended by emotional rather than intelligent statements. A dynamic faith rests on deepening insights, continuous search for facts and tested beliefs, worthful accomplishments, and cumulative results over long periods of time. It is a mark of superficial sentimentality, laziness, or fearful ignorance if one treasures a belief or a custom as so sacred that it cannot be examined for its truth and adequacy. All knowledge is based on incomplete data and tentative judgments; and, as in science, history, philosophy, and other areas of investigation so in religion we ought ceaselessly to welcome further explorations and revised findings. In fact, the religious quest can never be separated from the search for knowledge in all areas of life; for whatever adds to our understanding of man, the world in which we live, and the possibilities of a better life for more people—those factors are involved in a spiritual interpretation of life and in the effort to realize our growing ideals.

8. *Integration of experiences into a working philosophy of life.*— In this type of religious experience people are endeavoring to put together the atomistic, conflicting, contrasting, and partially understood incidents and events of ongoing life, so that they may have general working principles and stabilizing concepts. One faces the problems of good and evil, justice and injustice, joy and suffering, success and frustration, vitality and death, and the other contrasting experiences so

unevenly distributed among people, and one asks what the working principles are which make life intelligible and worthy of one's best efforts. One seeks goals, norms for conduct, enduring values, and integrating concepts by which to steer one's course and to measure one's progress. Generalizations may begin in the early organismic adjustments of a child as he learns to differentiate between kinds of things which give satisfaction and those which do not. As one grows older, language helps one to be objective regarding experiences, to hold in mind and to recall varied outcomes, and to formulate judgments as to relative values and best ways of attaining desired ends. One may be both critical and creative in organizing experiences and in working co-operatively with others for basic meanings and values. Religious principles must be based upon more than an outstanding happening or coincidence or more than a logical development of an unverified assumption. Life is full of unsolved problems, and the field of religion and morals has as large a number as any other. It is extremely difficult to get working principles of right and wrong, of what is the best thing under given circumstances, and of how to harmonize conflicting duties. We have the perennial questions as to why some suffer and others escape, why the wicked prosper and the righteous beg for bread, and why the sun shines on both the just and the unjust. Many other general and specific problems of religion and ethics multiply at all age levels and among all people. Religious education may begin with concrete situations, teach people to analyze the factors affecting outcomes, to identify the consequences for human welfare, and to work out principles for the general good and for the immediate situation; or it may impose certain assumed principles of conduct and action seeking conformity to abstract good. It will be remembered that Jesus found difficulty in applying authoritarian rules and declared his independence, "Ye have heard it said of old time, but I say....." In most cases it is necessary to penetrate deeper than generalities go, to work out a rational basis even if it involves a compromise with an abstract ideal. Religious attitudes and acts arise in an integration of experience on as high a level as circumstances permit, with an endeavor to improve limiting conditions.

9. *Appreciation of historical continuity.*—Religion is something more than an individual's impression of truth or sense of duty. It is a product of social interaction, the result of reflection upon one's own experiences and upon what others can communicate of theirs in matters of cosmic meanings and universal principles of conduct. Each generation should build on the achievements of preceding ones, using the lessons of the past to save repetition of errors and tragedies. The Bible, religious and general history, biography, poetry, fiction, and other records of human experience provide stimulating materials for critical creative thought. If wisely taught, a growing person will become acquainted with a wealth of spiritual records, depicting the rise and fall of individuals, groups, and nations. It is unfortunate when religious education is limited to Bible study; for the revelation of truth is understood better in the light of the records of all nations and of all periods of history. Curriculums for a well-graded program should draw from the richly varied resources of past and present. In interpreting the many different forms of religion and in working out a philosophy equal to the problem of the present, people need a sense of the developmental nature of religion and of its complex character. At each age level stories are needed of worthy living and also of striking contrasts of high and low conduct, providing opportunities to analyze typical problems of personal-social behavior. The ability to think religiously, to evaluate concepts and conduct, and to formulate significant goals, depends upon a well-organized body of ideas and a keen sense of trends which assure worth-while attainments. A feeling of stability and hopefulness involves a sense of historical continuity, a conditioning of individual or group faith by cumulative racial experience. Many of the fears and fantasies of people in matters of religion might be corrected if there were a better appreciation of how religious ideas and beliefs have arisen and have changed in times past. Many so-called "intuitions" are but echoes of ancient ideas which someone has

resurrected and sounded again. The past gives us both useful and handicapping ideas, which must be carefully weighed to be of value and to give enlightenment to the present.

10. *Participation in group celebrations.*—Religion has always had its times, places, and ceremonies for celebrating its highest values and for keeping its central beliefs and goals in the focus of attention. Worship in many forms has been a special way of gaining social-mindedness and emotional commitment to group ideas and ideals. All kinds of celebrations have possibilities of religious, educational, and motivating value; for they serve to recall critical events, to examine losses and gains, to develop group loyalties, and to indicate desirable lines of advance. To the degree that birthdays, community anniversaries, patriotic days, weddings, funerals, Sundays, graduations, initiations, and other special events are used to give meaning and directional guidance for worthy living they have spiritual significance. In times of group celebration people tend to become expansive, to get larger perspectives, to feel the norms of social approval, and to receive impetus to live more worthily. It is unfortunate when holidays and festivities degenerate into times of merely emotional excitation, amusement, and trivial activities. Homes can make birthdays and anniversaries occasions for group unification, individual recognition, welcoming of friends, and enrichment of relationships. Schools may use entertainments of various kinds, holiday observances, community rallies, exhibits, and graduation ceremonies as times for exalting standards of good citizenship and for giving group support to desirable forms of conduct. In churches there are weddings, funerals, youth rallies, installations, dedications, and special services of many kinds, in addition to the regular Sunday services, at which times it is possible vividly to present some of the high purposes and achievements of religious living.

For the majority of the people life is ordinarily drab, monotonous, a weary round of duties; so that they need the thrill of experiences out of the ordinary and a sense of belonging to a significant group. Celebrations mean appreciations, wholehearted expressions of pent-up desires; and they need not be hysterical or irrational, or merely formal gestures of polite approval. One reason many resort to liquor or to artificial stimulants of enthusiasm is that they have not learned to enjoy the use of intelligent, artistic, creative forms of expression. A celebration has a religious quality when it gives incentive to discriminating, co-operative commitment to a worthy cause or course of living. Whether it is a service of worship, a festival, or a more modest celebration, there is need for planning, for meaningful forms of expression, for recall of significant achievements, and for projection of purposes and practical procedures to give outlet to enlarged and refined desires.

In the following chapters we give varied illustrations of how these functional factors of religion may be furthered in the total life of the community, to the end of stirring new visions as to the place and possibilities of better-organized religion in our modern life. Spiritual qualities may be blocked, or released, by the conditions which prevail in one's environment, but by careful educational planning they may be intelligently and co-operatively cultivated. The urgent needs of mankind in every land challenge the religious forces to reorientate themselves, to evaluate the spiritual leaven at work in different agencies, and to unite all men and women of good will to work for a better world order. Children, youth, and adults need this energizing, integrating, functional understanding of religion, with a specific appreciation of the many institutions and people contributing toward its fulfilment.

One important value in using a functional analysis such as the foregoing rather than a theological or biblical orientation is that there is a normal basis for integrating religion into general education. The divisive nature of sectarianism is transcended by putting major attention upon the spiritual values and relationships of daily living instead of upon theories of deity and controversial theological doctrines. Prolonged studies in the public schools, and at higher levels of education, have shown that it is quite feasible to identify, at all age levels, both positive and negative factors affecting the growth of ideas, attitudes, and habit patterns herein described as religiously significant. Further, there is no difficulty in getting co-operation from general educators in furthering these ends; for they readily recognize these functional factors as central qualities wanted in education for democratic living. In one conference with public school teachers where this point of view was presented, a leading educator, from a state that emphasized separation of church and state, remarked that this was the first time that he knew he could be a teacher and a Christian at the same time. This functional approach, when well understood, makes it possible for teachers with varied religious background to give due attention to spiritual elements in all phases of their work without violating either the spirit or letter of our national Constitution. Religion may be perceived and developed as a normal evaluating attitude in all experiences.

Chapter Three

Sense of Worth and Social Sensitivity

IN THIS chapter we begin a series of illustrations of these ten basic experiences, with the purpose of making plain the important and pervasive character of these constituent elements of religion and of indicating the complex processes involved. Ordinary life is not dramatic, though it has exciting moments; and the reader does not need to expect anything unusual or bizarre in this portrayal. Yet, if one's imagination is equal to appreciation of what is happening in the lives of growing persons, there may be many thrills and chills in thinking over possibilities. There are dangers at every turn, but the development of intelligent, self-disciplined human beings cannot be achieved without incurring the risks of tragedies. In fact, we would not consider them tragedies if it were not for the alternative of a charming personality in each case. The development of personalities, and the growth of a world of harmoniously related people is surely a divine enterprise, a plan and a purpose that stagger the most daring mind. While the changes that take place in the growth of the simplest forms of plants and animals are so wonderful that they elicit deep reverence for the power that guides the processes, there should be an even more serious and worshipful reverence when one considers the marvelously complex processes producing self-conscious, intelligent, creative human beings. Let no one think that the functionalist is irreverent, or atheistical, because he does not worship ancient images or take major delight in formal ceremonies; for he has found a greater satisfaction in discovering "God" at work in his world and in sharing in the "divine" process. Religious education ceases to be a way of combating evil and of making people good by the magic of words and becomes an intelligent use of the divine laws of growth. To identify and to describe the factors and laws of this developmental process is to invite parents, teachers, and others who influence growing lives to co-operate in a more effective and comprehensive program of religious education.

Illustrations are drawn from all age levels, but particular attention is given to the formative years of childhood and youth. The temptation has been to high-light striking anecdotes, but to do this would defeat our primary purpose of calling attention to the ever present factors, positive and negative, shaping a growing life. The writer has made many special studies, preparatory to this writing, and has a great deal of data relative to the factors and processes described, but the longer he works on this problem of spiritual development the more he is impressed with the extraordinary character of what is usually treated as ordinary, and ignored. It may be difficult for some to dissociate religion from the realm of vague, mystical, and supernatural traditions; but once the functional point of view is assumed, the old forms of religion are better understood and the present character and operations of religion are appreciated. Whether this particular ten-point analysis is accepted is unimportant, but the need for analytical researches is urgent. Society has given many millions of dollars to research in the study of plants and animals, in attempts to improve industrial techniques, and in efforts to produce implements of war. Can we reasonably expect as careful study of ways to improve the quality of human living? The representative situations presented hereunder are taken from observations of children and of youth in school, home, and playground; from personal and directed studies of youth and adults; and from wide readings in the fields of psychology and education. At one time the writer spent six months in an intensive observational study of children in school, from the nursery to the sixth grade. It is hoped that the brief sampling record presented here may stimulate special researches in varied situations and with people of different age levels.

In directing attention to these specific factors the writer assumes that the reader will recognize that these are never isolated in actual life but are vital parts of a complex process. When a chemist tells us that there is oxygen in every drop of water, he does not forget that every atom of oxygen is inseparably related to hydrogen as long as we consider the nature of water. We focus attention on one element at a time better to understand the character of the interrelated elements. And in selecting our "typical" experiences we do not pretend to set forth exemplary patterns. It is impossible to suggest in these brief records why one child responds favorably to a given set of conditions and another is negative or frustrated. All that can be done is to give examples of situations where meaningful responses are taking place, and further study will be necessary to discover the exact combination suitable to a particular person's needs. It is taken for granted that what these records mean to readers will depend upon their familiarity with psychological analyses, their religious point of view, and their understanding of an educational process.

These basic experiences are presented in pairs, following the order of listing given in the previous chapter. This is done for the sake of clarity rather than of essential relationship. Any two could have been related, and ultimately all are expected to be interrelated. It might have been possible and desirable to take representative home, school, church, community, or other kinds of situations and have shown the interrelated factors; and it is hoped that readers will test out the reality and practicality of this ten-point analysis by so doing. We begin with "sense of worth" and "social sensivity," in order to show what we mean by these as continuous pervasive factors of spiritual growth in growing persons.[1]

SENSE OF WORTH

Sense of worth begins in infancy and is affected by an endless chain of events throughout the whole of life. One child is welcome in the home where he is born, and another is not wanted. One has the continual support of friendly people, while another battles with hostile forces. One is treated as a person with latent interesting capacities and is encouraged to express himself as a significant individual, while another is handled impersonally, filled with fears, and made to conform to the demands of others. Every well-written biography reveals factors which released, repressed, or guided latent possibilities. Some people master handicaps by a successful combination of personal and environmental resources, while others fail to achieve anything significant owing to an unfortunate combination of circumstances. Sense of worth, purposes, and attainments above the animal and mechanistic levels are the resultants of interplay of personal and environmental factors.

Nursery schools have proved of distinct value to many parents, especially to those who have only one child or when a child has no playmates of his own age. They provide a richer variety of opportunities than the ordinary home can give for development of self-confidence, independence, and a balanced sense of worth. Growth along these lines is related to such routine experiences as the following: learning to take off and to put on clothes, managing one's toilet needs, choosing activities for free play, adjusting to conflicts with one's peers, mastering shyness, overcoming fears of certain activities, gaining recognition by one's playmates, and gaining special rights and privileges because of worthy behavior. Progress is uneven and in one or two limited fields at a time. Three-year-olds tend to show superiority over two-year-olds, and those longest in a school assume rights beyond newcomers. They feel growth in themselves by contrasts. One child is worried by neglect of his playmates, and another plays by himself, or with others, as his moods run. One walks into any situation with quiet confidence, and another hesitates to assert himself. One child's sense of worth and outreach for self-expression are organized in every muscle and impulse, while another has no sense of security, acceptability, or right to self-assertion.

By kindergarten age, children have developed a fair number of skills. They can talk freely, act independently, and use a wide range of materials to advantage. They are becoming able to weigh their experiences and to pass judgments on conduct. It is fascinating to watch a skilful teacher draw them out in informal conversations. One morning a teacher said to her group, "Your parents are coming to see me tonight, and they will want to talk over what you are doing. I wonder what I can tell them that you are learning." There were eager responses, "You can tell my father that I am learning to take care of myself"; "I'm learning to paint"; "I'm learning to clean up"; "I'm able to dress myself"; and one little fellow chimed in, "You can tell my parents I'm learning to fight." The teacher told the observer that the last lad had found it very difficult at first to hold his own but was now managing himself very well. He was not pugnacious, but he did not hesitate to defend his own rights. At home his parents had overprotected him, but at school he found he was expected to take care of himself.

Schoolteachers continually remind children that they are growing up, that more is expected of them, and that they must expect more of themselves. Yet too much of what is expected is regimentation, both at home and at school. They find little opportunity for free experimentation. One child confided that he was always found fault with by someone and continually scolded for whatever he did. Another of the same third grade told of interesting things he was doing at home, of the many things one could do at school, and of what he planned to do. In city apartments and in crowded schools there are not enough varied activities to stimulate growing capacities. To discover, and to cultivate, one's worth there is need of challenging opportunities, freedom, and pressure of social expectation.

Psychologists have noted for a long time that a fundamental desire is for recognition by one's associates. Both old and young will go to ridiculous extremes to get it. In a third-grade class, working on a unit about Holland, a girl was called on to answer a question. She replied, "The Dutch people do not wear shoes in their homes, and, by the way, my mother bought me a mink coat last year and a camel's hair coat this year." The teacher explained to the observer that the child came from a wealthy home but was left in charge of a maid most of the time. She seemed hungry for affection and attention and repeatedly made a nuisance of herself. In another room a teacher pointed out a boy who had been most bothersome but who was changed almost overnight by an improvement in his marks. The teacher had sensed his need, had commended him whenever she could, and had encouraged him in his work. As his class standing improved, he ceased to be a bother and took a pride in worthy achievements.

It is difficult to give due consideration for individual differences and for particular needs of members of a large class. Even in routine questioning it is hard to be fair to all. When hands go up, one child may be allowed to respond and, if able to do so satisfactorily, gets approval; but at the same time others have no like opportunity. In a fifth-grade class a lad in the front row kept waving his hand at every question. The teacher ignored him, until, suddenly, she turned on him, "Well, Billy, you answer!" The lad became self-conscious and nervous and stammered a poor reply. Instead of helping him gain composure to do his best the teacher rebuked him and humiliated him, "Every time your hand goes up. It's a crazy hand, the craziest I ever saw." The boy was hurt. He needed a different kind of teacher, and so did the rest in that room. Sense of worth is much more difficult for some to attain than for others, and the old biblical proverb still holds good, "He that hath, to him shall be given; and he that hath not, from him shall be taken away even that which he hath" (Luke 4:25).

Many injure others without thinking, though some take a delight in hurting others' feelings. A sixth-grade class of boys were playing around a swimming pool. The lads were of strongly contrasting heights, as is normal in a sixth grade, but small and large had been chumming together without respect to size. Thoughtlessly, the instructor lined them up, "Line up by size. You shorties get down where you belong." One could see them wince. Sense of worth had a bad jar. This instructor would not have hurt anyone purposely, but he frequently showed complete ignorance of how boys of this age struggle for status, especially those who are prepubescent and small for their age. On the other hand, he sometimes expected too much from a big overgrown lad. It is hard for growing youngsters to keep a balanced sense of worth in this rapidly changing period of pubescence, and they need sympathetic guidance by wise adults.

Overaggressiveness is a frequent fault in members of a minority group. They try to compensate for disparagement by proving superior skills or by displaying special loyalty, generosity, or bravado. Instead of gaining favorable approval, this often gives further occasion for prejudice and ill treatment. People of priviliged and majority groups can hardly appreciate the problems of those who are handicapped because of antipathies against race, color, nationality, creed, or economic standing. To be ostracized, or continually put at a disadvantage, makes it difficult to develop a well-rounded and attractive personality, and those who do succeed deserve generous credit.

But equal opportunities will not solve all problems; for there is a big difference in people's abilities to make use of opportunities. The observer found some high-school pupils complaining that they did not have any liberty, that they were "pushed around like cattle," that no one was allowed to think for himself. Yet in the same school and grades other students boasted of their school's progressive character, telling of how assignments were made so that one had all the freedom and chance for initiative that one could wish and describing the large measure of self-government in the general school program and in their clubs. Perhaps one reason for the common criticism of progressive education is that many students do not profit by freedom. They are victims of repression or of laissez faire, and they do not know how to discipline themselves and to use freedom to advantage. Before progressive education can do its best with the younger generation, a special program will have to be set up for parents and other adults in order that they may learn to appreciate the advantages of a psychological approach to a boy or girl rather than a blind, traditional one. A study made a few years ago by the writer, of high-school students, showed that the occasions which affect their sense of worth and ambitions were rated in the following order:

1. Those which give them opportunities to try themselves out and to compare themselves with others, such as, giving a talk before an audience, meeting emergencies when they come, taking responsibilities at home when parents are away, being trusted by a teacher to make a demonstration in class, meeting competition and winning a place, and earning money and paying one's expenses.

2. Successes and failures. "As went my grades so went my feelings of self-worth," said one boy. They have partial and chance measures of their capacities but no adequate standards or means of appraisal of abilities or possible attainments. They pay attention to such indices as these: marks in different subjects, winning a position on an athletic team or in a club, doing a task successfully and getting approval, and overcoming special handicaps.

3. Recognition by teachers and fellow-students. They are sensitive to criticisms of others, but enjoy favorable comments. They need a sense of security and worth independent of the fickle attitudes of others.

4. The example of others. Worthy examples may stimulate them, but it is impossible to know why different people appeal to different young people. They realize the fact that unworthy examples frequently influence them and that they are more sensitive to associates than to principles. They seem to have few opportunities to weigh the qualities and attainments of people and have no critical norms.

One of the most regrettable conditions found among young people was the lack of definite ambitions and purposes. They drifted along, with very little sense of duties or of obligations to make themselves assets in society. While there was some vocational and educational guidance, most were content to drift along, following lines of chance interest or those of least resistance. In one school about the only one who seemed to stir any feelings of social obligation was a good civics teacher, and pupils talked more of the after-class discussions than of the in-class studies. Few showed any feeling of social expectancy; few mentioned home, school, or church as giving them any incentive to prepare themselves for special tasks; few seemed to have any vision of opportunities for rich life-investment. When war came, many young people were influenced by the appeals to defend the world against those who would destroy democracy and freedom, and they gave intelligent response. There is no doubt that human needs could be presented in just as challenging, and far more attractive, forms for peacetime enlistment. They need to have more experiences in sharing in enterprises which have large human significance and to have more contacts with people who live interesting, unselfish lives. They need vision and faith—vision of what ought to be and can be done and faith strengthened by knowledge of people who are actually doing some of these important tasks.

One other quality that both young people and their elders seemed to lack in sense of worth was the ability to stand alone on a moral issue. Most tended to follow the crowd and to justify their attitudes and actions by the excuse, "Everybody does it." Few seemed to have any definite reason for deciding action on such matters as smoking, drinking, petting, petty gambling, late hours, profanity, or lying. Many seemed afraid to face criticism for appearing moral or religious, accepting the line of least resistance in any situation. In church circles some things are taboo, but the underlying principles seem vague. In gangs working principles vary, but no critical thinking seems to have determined them. Most young people lack the poise and inspiration of well-thought-out principles, ideals, and desirable lines of conduct. They need to be able to evaluate popular fashions, to meet censure, to use refined forms of behavior without appearing at all priggish.

For some people, sense of worth and purpose in life are associated with theological beliefs and teachings, and these are assumed to be primary forces in spiritual attainments. They are taught from early childhood that there is a God, a heavenly father, who made man in his own image, and that people have the right to be called sons of God. They are taught doctrines of salvation through faith in Jesus Christ and are led to believe in a mystical working of the Holy Spirit. These beliefs are taken literally by many people and symbolically by others but usually are the products of indoctrination and rationalization rather than of critical thought based upon empirical evidence. They function powerfully for some people and are justified on that score, but they lack relationship to the types of experience which we have been describing, failing to integrate the whole of life with basic working beliefs. Traditional forms of theology must give place to empirically and functionally based systems of unifying religious philosophy.

Without multiplying other descriptions of experiences contributing to growth of sense of worth and release of spiritual forces, let us briefly mention a number of other contrasting situations in which the possibilities of either positive or negative outcomes are suggested. Most people will have recurring ups and downs, but education seeks to reduce the waste of unprofitable experiences and to multiply the opportunities for enriching and stimulating responses. The following should cause the reader to recall many other like situations:

Attention of friendly people, or disparagement by hostile ones

Enjoyment of affection, or victim of hate

Being chosen for a leader, or being humiliated as an insignificant thing

Being an accepted and valued member of a group, or being ignored in a group

Feeling ability to win attention of someone of the opposite sex, or being treated disdainfully by such

Success in championing an unpopular cause, or feeling guilty of fear, or of failure to fulfil a moral duty

Feeling secure in one's job or profession, or feeling unequal to one's tasks and, consequently, insecure

Attaining substantial financial gains, or losing money and property through incompetency

Enjoying vigorous health, or feeling unable to meet the physical demands of
one's responsibilities
Miraculous deliverance from some calamity, or victim of some tragedy
Exaltation by some religious belief, or depression by loss of long-time faith

SOCIAL SENSITIVITY

Examples of this complementary correlative of sense of worth are
probably the easiest to identify of all our types of experience; for they
are the most commonly emphasized religious traits. Yet there are
many subtle factors in the growth of social sensitivity which are
undeveloped. It is easier to take the role of people in one's own social
group than of those of different class, race, nationality, religion, or
geographical location. One's attitudes toward others are affected un-
consciously by group prejudices, caricatures, generalizations, conflicting desires, and economic strains and fears. The ability to hold
self-interests and others' interests and needs in mind at the same
time and to keep them harmoniously related grows slowly, and some
people never master the skill. Only a few seem to be able to develop
this spiritual quality which combines humility with social power,
kindliness with respect, and magnanimity with naturalness. Yet the
measure of a personality depends upon the ability of one to identify
himself with others, the habit of so doing, and the experience of
many varied relationships.

For the first few years of life a child tends to be egocentric because
he is unable to be anything else. His growing mind is busy with
organizing his own affairs, and people are little more than things in
the environment. It is distinctly a forward step when he becomes able
to take the role of another person and to interrelate his own wishes
and acts with those of the other person. One does not, of course, become moral until this level of thinking and acting is reached, and he
does not become what may be called truly religious until there begins
a generalization moving toward universal standards of conduct. Even
if this is true, the religious educator is just as much interested in the
conditioning influences and adjustments of the little child at this stage

as later. A spiritual atmosphere is necessary for the finest development of spiritual qualities, and what an educator can do with the adults, and others around the child, is as important as anything that may be done directly to the child in the younger years. The baby needs affection, regular and consistent attention, freedom from overstimulation, and satisfaction in co-operative actions.

What a good kindergarten teacher can do to socialize children is illustrated by the transformation of a pair of twins in a public school class. The observer commented on the good behavior of the twin boys who were playing happily on the floor in the midst of piles of blocks with which other children were working. They were not disturbing anyone else's property, and they were managing themselves excellently. To a favorable commendation, the teacher replied, "You should have seen those little terrors three months ago. Their mother had been deserted by the father, and they were too much for her. They had gone wild, and the mother sent them to school to get rid of them for a few hours a day. At first, they acted like wild animals, without any self-control or consideration of others. Gradually, we have helped them to see the advantages of keeping to the rules of the class, considering others, and being co-operative." That teacher in the public schools had done far more for those youngsters than would have been possible in the once-a-week contacts of a Sunday school, and the change was just as spiritual as if it had occurred in a church.

Very little race or class consciousness is shown in the younger grades, but outside influences soon creep in, and youngsters reflect attitudes of older people. In a first-grade class two children were sitting at a small table. Suddenly, without any immediate occasion for the remark the boy said, "Catholics do not like Jews." The little girl opposite replied, "I'm a Jew. Don't you like me?" "Yes," he said, "I like you, but Catholics do not like Jews." The teacher who overheard the conversation tactfully invited them to come and play a game, and they went gladly together. The observer wondered when this might recur, what had caused the remark, and whether both might be victims of social prejudice in days ahead. The teacher waited for an opportune time to develop desirable mutual understandings.

A fourth-grade teacher told her class that one of the Negro attendants in the school had just taken some prizes for photographic work. She interested them in the excellent pictures he had made, and they asked whether they could invite him to come to their class to show some of his pictures. A committee was appointed to ask him, and the class learned to feel the possibilities of significant worth in one who was usually treated impersonally as a mere public servant.

In one home a mother slaved for her only child, expecting others to humor him and requiring very little of him. He had a hard time with his playmates and when he was ten was described as "a whining, temperamental youngster, never satisfied unless he was getting attention and could have his own way." In a neighboring home another child, born about the same time, was treated kindly and intelligently by both parents but was expected to adjust himself happily with others. He was encouraged when he acted socially and discouraged whenever he whined or fretted. Though the first child had more native ability, the latter soon excelled him in school and was welcome wherever he went. The first mother failed to appreciate the self-discipline necessary for an attractive, competent personality.

In the field of sex, wholesome attitudes are largely a matter of social sensitivity. They arise in shared interests which transcend merely sensual emotional excitation. They begin in childhood as boys and girls play together, learn to respect each other, and live in homes and social groups in which modesty and refinement are observed. When questions as to physiological differences arise, or as problems of reproduction become of interest, they are answered in a frank and respectful way. As the adolescent age introduces new problems of adjustment and understanding, young people need good books to read on matters of sex, family life, and social responsibility, with opportunities to talk over questions with persons with whom they have normal relationships and in whom they have confidence. Ideals need to be stimulated and a stigma aroused against sex debasement and obscenity. Though churches have tended to condemn dancing, more intelligent and liberal attitudes are becoming prevalent; and it is interesting to discover that many people find dancing one of their most satisfying forms of recreation. They need to develop standards of good taste, to have a wide variety of interests, and to share in activities in which intellectual and aesthetic creative talents are matched and given social expression. They need to face the facts of sex perversion, sex inequalities, family discords, and also the constructive measures that are being developed to offset these.

Some homes give children a good start in right relations to other people by the exemplary attitudes of the parents both within and outside the home circle. Churches idealize the spirit of friendliness and social justice and stimulate interests and participation in various kinds of social causes. But it is the public school in its social studies which deals most thoroughly and intelligently with the manifold phases of human relationships in the modern world. However, there is too much separation of theory and practice in social education, for verbal discussions do not take the place of firsthand contacts with other people in critical situations and practical adjustments must meet mutual needs. Both churches and schools are trying to provide projects in which children and youth may share, which have significant meaning and value in local, national, and international relationships. One high-school lad said, "My most satisfactory participations in school or community life have been in clubs which have had social and charitable purposes to benefit the school, community, or some charitable organization."

Other types of experience developing social interests or stimulating serious thought include the following:

Movies given in the school showing how other people live
Movies and lectures describing important social projects in industry or government

Talks given in assemblies by persons representing important social movements
Campaigns to interest support of Red Cross work
Committees to improve social relations in the school
Debates in a civics class on community, national, or international social issues
Reading reports on labor arbitrations
Observation of courtesy week, and talks by teachers on good manners
Taking responsibility for success of a school function
Seniors given responsibility for helping in freshman week
Having a part in a student council dealing with student problems
Listening to a round-table discussion on race or other problems of adjustment
Earning money by doing janitor work and seeing things from a janitor's viewpoint
Helping to create public sentiment to improve school equipment

Every day on the radio and in the press are many illustrations of situations in which the rights and needs of people are at stake, problems which should be considered sympathetically and constructively by young people and adults. Many different agencies are working on these, some entirely unrelated to organized religion; and yet all these movements have distinctly religious qualities. Participation in these may yield a religious experience, and the church should encourage intelligent, sympathetic, and critical interest in such community and national enterprises. Whatever credit should be given to organized religious institutions for making people sensitive to spiritual values, we have to admit that many people do not learn them from the church, nor do they always find satisfactory outlet for their ideals through church-directed enterprises. It is more important to identify growing elements of the religious spirit wherever found and to whatever degree developed than to try to channel all righteousness through a church system. We need to welcome any advance of the human spirit even if its leaders will not describe their principles or goals in theological terms.

The following brief references to current social issues will illustrate how our first two basic religious experiences are involved, what opportunities are needed for people to realize their fullest worth, and what actions are necessary to prove that one has brotherly love and is his brother's keeper, or, in our terms, that one has social sensitivity:

1. The outstanding social problem of our age is in the field of international relations, and the movement which represents the highest spiritual attainment in this area to date is the United Nations Charter. In this the welfare of the people of the earth has been considered without respect to race, nationality, creed, or other traditional forms of separation. Its goals, its main proposals, and the spirit which dominates its councils, express religious idealism. Religion must transcend its conventional institutions and work through governments, courts, schools, and social and economic organizations if the world is to enjoy peace, freedom, and progress.

2. Perhaps the second greatest problem and movement for human rights is the growing demand for racial equality. It is a world ferment and one that has many different forms in different countries. It is an exceedingly difficult problem for vested interests are imperiled, irrational but deeply emotional feelings of superiority are irritated, and many "superiors" are unable or unwilling to adjust themselves to the inescapable facts of change. The dangers of mob action keep many communities in constant fear; for irresponsible agitators are active to keep unrest stirred. There is need for education, for specific changes allowing more equal rights and privileges, and for co-operative planning and action based upon careful studies. In America the complex phases of the Negro problem have been well studied by a Swedish economist and are reported in the two volumes of *An American Dilemma.* This was done at the invitation of American groups working on this tension situation. Dr. Gunnar Myrdal reviews conditions in both the North and South, states the evident needs for improvement, tells of progress that has been made, and outlines what seems to be the hope for the future. In this struggle for human rights the churches have done a great deal, but other agencies have done more, and changes will be achieved only as co-operative action of labor groups, reform organizations, local- and federal-government agencies,

school, and churches prove the sincerity of attitudes and policies. This is primarily a problem of spiritual growth in which mutual respect and co-operative living are the normal expression.

In the world situation, whites are beginning to realize that they are outnumbered by colored peoples and that there is a growing resentment against their assumptions of superiority and their claims for higher privileges. The Japanese war was undoubtedly due in large part to this feeling. The Chinese millions will never settle down again satisfied with an ancient cultural standard of living. The people of India will not be content until white control is overthrown and they govern themselves. The colored races of Asia, Africa, and the islands of the seas, as well as those who are settled in every country of the world, have become conscious of their rights, possibilities, and power. It will take more than prayers, songs, and mission funds to solve these problems. The irrepressible demands of people for better status and for larger privileges is a spiritual urge, and the response must reflect appreciation and magnanimity. The hope for a united world and for peaceful progress rests in the increasing amount of intelligent good will and changing policies of organizations and governments. Religious people must recognize something more basic and persistent than strategic appeasement in the actions of governments, in the adjustments of mission boards, and in the tones of radio and press. Deep spiritual forces are at work, and radical changes are taking place in every land. Statesmen, religious leaders, educators, and molders of the public mind everywhere need to be men of vision, wisdom, and deep spiritual understanding.

3. Economic questions interpenetrate all social relationships and require spiritual interpretation. There cannot be peace and good will where hunger and starvation dwell, and there will not be enduring peace until a sense of economic justice prevails. In the war-ravaged countries millions suffer, and for years the resources of the civilized world will be strained to meet these needs. The United Nations Charter provides machinery for international economic co-operation,

but its effective working depends upon an unselfish spirit of internationalism that springs from the hearts of the common people. Governments cannot do much unless homes, schools, and churches develop the sense of human values and common rights. An American Congress may vote down appropriations for a Fair Employment Practices Committee, but it cannot crush the growing spirit which gave it birth. Great corporations may try to protect their interests without consideration for human needs or for dangers of bloody conflicts; but the tide has turned, and the forces of spiritual progress will not be stopped. The religious educator, as well as the general educator, needs to teach young people and adults rightly to appraise these social forces in order that they may intelligently and effectively support those which give best promise of permanent worth. They should inspire young people to see the opportunities for furtherance of spiritual ends by taking responsible part in such movements as co-operatives, labor education, voters' leagues, economic reform, international good will, and ecumenical church conferences. Leaders are needed in government, in the teaching field, in business, in radio and journalism, and in many other fields of modern life to clarify thinking in economic adjustments and to keep human values to the fore.

4. As religion has developed into its higher forms, it has taken a large interest in relief of human suffering and in the promotion of good health for all. The spirit of the Good Samaritan has been taken as the standard of neighborliness, and the Red Cross has carried its services to every land. Hospitals have been built, charitable agencies have dispensed relief, visiting nurses have gone into slums, and in later years many types of health insurance and medical protection have been organized. Yet it is strange that even in the medical profession, which has been outstanding in its services to the needy and which has had high codes of professional ethics, fears and selfish interests have been aroused to block social advances. Strong organizations fight proposals for compulsory health insurance and social security measures that would bring protection to millions who cannot

now have proper medical care. In spite of opposition and misrepresentation, the movement goes forward in America and in other countries; and many medical men of highest rank champion this larger socialization of medicine. Another large field opens up for young people to invest their lives in research, public health services, rehabilitation of the handicapped, nursing, and the varied departments of medical service. At one time the church limited its label for religious service in this field of human service to the medical missionary, and even he had to do evangelistic work of a conventional kind to qualify. Today religion is challenged to prevent medicine from degenerating in to a field of human mechanics or a commercialized professional combine. Religion must spiritualize all phases of this noble profession or retire from the field of human needs. And what it needs to do in this profession should be done in all professions and vocations.

5. Without elaborating any other areas of social sensitivity, let us list a few more of the critical situations where a lack of religion endangers society and where promising advances of its transforming spirit give hopes for a better world:

Governmental control of prices and distribution of goods when scarcity threatens the common welfare

The battle between private interests and public in matters of such general needs and resources as are represented in the Tennessee Valley Authority and other like projects

The struggle between capitalism and socialism as systems of social operation involving freedom, incentives to highest forms of living, and the common good of mankind

Employment and wages, with a decent standard of living, security, and a voice in management.

Understanding of the personal and social effects of drinking alcoholic beverages, with needs for education, control of industry, and development of higher values

Development of recreational interests which will refuse debasing forms and exalt refined creative arts and skills

Compulsory military training in peacetime in a democracy and in a world trying to organize international security

Prevention of child labor, with fair opportunities for education in all sections of a country

Problems of juvenile delinquency, preventive measures in social case work, corrective institutions, and related educational programs and recreational provisions

Social controls on the press, censorship in war and peace, sources of news, sense of social responsibility

Monopolies in business, restraint of trade, private or public control of production, prices, and distribution

Housing, restricted areas, slum clearance, rural needs, crowded city conditions, privacy.

Care for the handicapped in society—crippled, blind, deaf, mentally deficient, neurotic and psychotic cases, chronic ailments, infectious diseases

Improvement of education, common learnings for democratic needs, citizenship, vocational training, health and physical education, program for leisure time, distribution of costs, teacher-training

Everyone of the above situations suggests plenty of reasons for pessimism and defeatism, but in every dark picture there is a ray of light; for the religious ferment is at work everywhere. It is foolish to say that human nature is hopelessly bankrupt, that Christianity has never been tried, or that man must wait for some supernatural deliverance. The forces of redemption are in the growth processes of normal life, and religion is but the discovery, exaltation, and use of these. Revelations of the "divine" nature are not to be thought of as limited to "unique" manifestations in history and to specially chosen people but are to be recognized in the totality of ongoing life. Every reference to God as an integrating, creative, personality-producing power should have factual evidence to support the claim. The functional view of religion, which we are describing and illustrating, gives proof of this pervasive regenerating power at work, but the concepts are larger and more comprehensive of experience than the old anthropomorphic forms. In the following chapters we focus our spotlight on other phases of religion, but they are vitally related to our first two categories; and they, too, suggest the possibilities of an expanding program of religious education.

Chapter Four

Appreciations and Discriminations

THE illustrations and discussions of this chapter deal directly and realistically with types of experience about which much philosophical and theological speculation and controversy have centered. We deal first with the facts about the universe and its processes which have led to beliefs in spirits and deities, including the many variations of the Hebrew-Christian concepts of God. We ask whether religion rests primarily upon appreciations of the nature, laws, and discovered resources of the universe or upon theories of a deity and man's relations to that mental construct. In our study of the nature and processes of the universe we are faced with the fact that this universe is one in which there are plural possibilities of development and that man is an agent with large freedom, able to appreciate the processes, to understand the different alternatives of life, and to work discriminatingly and creatively. Further, we find that the centuries reveal that man as a free, self-conscious being has to take the consequences of his choices and acts. As a being capable of intellectual growth and responsibility, he must learn by experience and must realize his maximum possibilities by intelligent co-operative relationship to the creative and constructive forces and resources of life.

In the course of his development, man has tried many times to escape from this rigorous discipline, and the religions of the world reflect his desires and his imaginative solutions. An almost unbelievable variety of imaginary spirits and deities have been pictured as governing and controlling powers in the universe; and with each imaginary construct, men have concocted ways of maintaining friendly relations and of escaping from consequences of misdeeds. The Hebrew-Christian tradition has seen a continuous revision of theories, from the early ideas of tribal gods and placating sacrifices to the latest creations of modern theologians or emotional preachers. All have been declared revelations, and all have been accepted as very real, except by critical and questioning minds of each generation. Men will never cease to speculate upon the nature of the controlling and creative power, or powers, transcendent or immanent in the forces and processes of the universe. They will continue to revise the philosophies and theologies of the past and to try to build new and better ones. It is inevitable, and it is desirable.

The principle which we emphasize, and which underlies the whole purpose of this book, is that adequate religious education can never be an indoctrination into any particular theology, fundamentalist or liberal, but must rest upon the primary experiences and growing appreciations of life itself. Images manufactured by the Moody Bible Institute, the Federated Theological Faculties of the University of Chicago, or any of the hundreds of Protestant, Catholic, Jewish, and other institutions of America, Europe, or other countries of the world, are only images, whatever their maker. Religion needs to rest upon primary experiences of the world and its processes, upon growing and continually revised appreciations of its realities, values, and possibilities. Religion should integrate the whole of experience, instead of dividing it into sacred and secular parts or of treating it dualistically as natural and revealed religion. It can do this by freeing itself from the limitations of theological imagery, critically evaluating all experience and seeking to conserve and to develop the highest values of all personal-social living. The qualities of religion and the needs for spiritual adjustment pervade all phases of individual and collective life. We seek a program of religious education which shall begin in the youngest child and which may unify the constructive factors of growing experience into a stabilizing and energizing faith.

In taking this naturalistic and functional approach we find it necessary repeatedly to emphasize the fact that we have not done away with anything that was real or vital in the familiar theological concepts of God, sin, salvation, Jesus Christ, will of God, spirit of Christ, eternal life, prayer, forgiveness, sacrifice, Bible, Word of God, revelation, inspiration, sanctification, heaven, hell, supernatural, sacred, or holy. In the ten areas of our functional analysis, and particularly in these two, "appreciation of the universe" and "discrimination in values," we deal directly and fearlessly with the facts of life and the best meanings that twentieth-century accumulated learnings can present to us. We face the thousands of varieties of theological ideas, with the tremendous assortment of images and with people pathetically trying to believe in the traditions into which they have been indoctrinated, and we seek a religion that represents the underlying urges of all these which can unify the faith and outreaches of all mankind. We seek a clearer understanding of that reality, or process, in our universe which men have tried through the ages to picture and have called by many different names, and in appreciation we include a growing co-operative relationship. We seek salvation from all that degrades and handicaps man's upward climb, in order that he may be enabled to realize his fullest possibilities, and we expect this to be achieved by discriminatory sacrificial obedience to the laws of spiritual growth written in the very nature of the universe and in man's nature. There are common ends in all forms of religion, and these ends are the maximum functioning of all human beings as growing, intelligent, discriminating persons.

APPRECIATION OF THE UNIVERSE

In order to aid in identifying the types of experience which we include under this heading we suggest that attention be directed to the following elements in the situations described at different age levels and in varying life relations:

1. Experiences which give one a sense of order, stability, dependable forces, and discoverable laws in the structure and processes of one's world and which call forth desires to be co-operative, law-abiding, and intelligent.
2. Experiences which uncover the growing possibilities of life, the inexhaustible resources of the universe, the creative forces continually at work and which inspire creative sustained effort and desire to share in large enterprises related to human good.
3. Experiences which give one a sense of the relativity of all events in the great all-comprehensive scheme of the universe and of the ages, which develop meanings for the interrelatedness of all things, and which stir desire for understanding of basic comprehensive principles as well as working norms for conduct.
4. Experiences which give one a sense of man's place in the universe, his capacity to function in relation to universal forces and to all members of the human family, with growing desires to be a worthy member of the human family, realizing with others increasing values and achievements.
5. Continual re-evaluation of ideas, attitudes, and acts in the light of growing experience and in the light of the experiences and interpretations of others of the past and present with opportunities for co-operative meditation, planning, and action.

The beginnings of appreciation for an orderly world and satisfying adaptation to it are found in the earliest experiences of infancy. If a child's feeding, sleeping, and routine care are governed by a well-regulated schedule, his organism will become adjusted to this before his mind is able to understand its meaning. But if, when he cries, someone rushes to attend him and he has no regularity for feeding or care except as response to a cry, he has no basis for appreciation of system and order. He may grow up feeling that he is the center of the world and that he can, and has a right to, swing the universe to suit his wants. Some adults seem to have grown up that way and even picture a deity whose duty it is to adjust the universe at their demand. A wartime news item told of a chaplain on a warship praying for fine weather as the fleet moved into action so that the thousand planes could better destroy the enemy. The reporter testified, "His prayer has been heeded." It is strange how many people associate God's action with the coincidental outcomes of a wish or prayer. If a child has the good fortune to start in an orderly home and, as he grows, learns to differentiate between order and chaos in home arrangements, play conditions, school life, and the many other situations of his widening world, he may come to appreciate the marvelous system and dependable order of the processes of his universe. He will not be satisfied with any theological teaching of a deity who can interrupt this order at any time to please a particular individual or nation whom it favors.

Nature limits the sensitivities and comprehensions of a child so that the complexities of his world do not overwhelm him. He learns slowly and gradually puts things together in systems and relationships so that meanings and associations for symbols are quite different from those of mature adults. A five-year-old was told that the earth was like the map globe and that people lived on all sides of the earth. He puzzled with the idea, wondering how people on the underside could hang on, but finally settled it by saying, "Perhaps it's like fairyland." A second-grade boy brought a drawing to show the writer when he was visiting a public school class. It was a rough drawing with a dark blue background and gold stars, sun, and moon pasted on. Asked how far he thought the sun was from the earth, he replied, "About ten thousand feet, I guess." Asked further about the moon and stars, he said the moon was about the same distance away but probably the stars were a little farther away. Pointing to the blue sky of the drawing, the visitor said, "And what's in the sky?" The boy named clouds, dust, rain, and snow; and, when he was questioned, "Anything else?" he hesitated a moment and then started, "Oh, yes! God is there, and Jesus, and the Virgin Mary, and Saint Joseph, and lots of saints." The lad came from a Catholic church which had some interesting murals, and he tried to put school and church learnings together.

How fantastic and unorganized are the ideas of the world into which children have to fit common teachings of an omniscient, omnipotent, and omnipresent, personal God is indicated by answers of fifth- and sixth-grade children to the request of their teacher that they should write out what they thought the universe was like. When the teacher wrote the assignment on the board, half the class, in each case, raised their hands; and someone asked, "Please, teacher, what does that word mean?" The only explanation given was a gesture with the arms and the reply, "You know what that word 'universe' means— the great big world in which we live. Tell me what it is like." The following are typical answers:

FIFTH GRADE

I think the universe is a large mass of air with space where there is no air. It also has the earth, sun, moon, and other planets. Science thinks that no people live on any other planet, but I think people could live even if there were no air.

The universe is made up of masses of land and gases. Each mass of land is a planet and has a name. They are named after gods and goddesses. Scientists believe that men once lived on Mars, but they are not sure.

I appreciate the sun which is a part of the universe. If there were no sun we would probably freeze to death. The sun and moon hold up the earth by gravity.

I think the earth is the best place for humans to live, but I may be wrong. I like to live on the earth and I wouldn't live anywhere else.

I think the universe is like a big hollow ball, with the stars, planets, space, and air in it. It is so large you could go a million miles a second and never reach the outside.

The universe is a big mass of gases. Near the earth the air is mostly oxygen and nitrogen. The air is held near the earth by its gravity. In this mass of gases there are very large masses of soil and rocks which are called land. Compared to the hole universe they are pretty small.

Before God created the trees, birds, and many planets the universe was a mass of land, water, and air. There were know people on the earth. God wanted the land to have beauty. It took God six days and nights and on the seventh he rested. That is how the Bible says the universe was made.

I am glad we have our place in the universe because we are about in the middle, and we have a good view of all the other planets and stars. Gravity holds us all in our places.

SIXTH GRADE

There is no end to the universe. It is made up of many stars, a few planets, and some comets. Power probably makes it go. Gravitation probably keeps it together. It is like a motor keeping everything under control. Planets may have vegetation and living things on them.

I guess the universe is round. In the middle is the sun, and around it are the planets, then space, and different stars, and then more space. It starts nowhere and ends nowhere. There might be people like us on the other planets, or they might be different. They might be on the moon, or even on the sun. As for god, or gods, or spirits, I think there is someone who guides us. As to the age of the earth or how it came, I do not think it is like what is described in the Old Testament. The early people made up stories and the Bible is a collection of stories.

I think the universe is a ball with stars around it, and the sun going around all of it. The universe does not move but the sun does. I think God made the universe.

The universe is created things viewed as one system. The wind or the air makes it go. The moist climate keeps it together. It is round. The relation of God is a jewish idea.

I believe the universe is made up of many plantits that cannot be counted. It is like ball bearings that keep going around each other. An unseen chain probably holds them together. I think God put the earth together.

I think the universe is round because the earth is round, and so are the sun and the moon, and the plannits. Gravity keeps it together and the air keeps them from bumping together. I think there are angels in the universe, and all the Bible people. God guards us and wants to help us in time of need.

A trip to a planetarium did not help much to clear up ideas of the universe. It is too big a concept even for most adults. And what a personal God means in the processes of this vast array of heavenly bodies, stretching out in space for distances only describable in terms of light years and developing in time for probably millions of years, very few adults have tried to state. Yet many speak fluently about God as if his operations were no more complex than those of the commander-in-chief of the Allied forces in World War II. Their inability to comprehend complex processes is much like that of the little three-year-old girl whose grandmother had returned home after a visit. When she received a letter from her, she said to her mother, "Why doesn't grandma bring her own letter instead of sending it by a postman?" The distance of two thousand miles and means of communication were not understood.

Once adults pass the stage of thinking of God as a big man in the skies who is kind and sentimental, who likes to hear children and grown-ups sing his praises, religion may mean something more than saying, "Thank you, God." It will begin in the response of a child's organism to tender care, to rhythmic and harmonious sounds, to good food, to freedom, and to opportunities for quiet, regular rest, because the organism grows best and finds satisfactions under such conditions. Even when the child becomes able to talk of his experiences, to compare favorable and unfavorable situations and reactions, the organic response underlies verbal expression of thought. The religious education of the child would then involve provision of many opportunities to experience the essential qualities of the natural processes in home, school, church, and community relationships. Any reference to God as a symbol of unity, creativity, growth, personality-producing power, love, beauty, or other universally recognized good inherent in the world in which man lives, moves, and has being would come as persons were able to perceive these pervasive qualities and to feel their value for increasing meanings and possibilities of personal-social living. The main thing from a functional point of view is that people should discover the resources for, and principles of abundant living and that they should intelligently and wholeheartedly respond to their privileges and responsibilities. The utilization of theological terms is secondary; but, as language is important for reflection and social action, a certain amount of theology is inevitable at all stages of growth.[1]

Appreciation of order and orderly living comes gradually as experiences of the values of such are multiplied in matters of hunger, sleep, relations with other people, conditions for health, and general understanding of the sequences of causes and effects. One of the things which hinders quick and easy perception of law and order is the fact that there is never exact repetition of any event; for change and variety are as much a part of nature as dependability. Nothing is static. There is always something new and interesting. Though day and night follow each other regularly, one may always expect variety in each, and in every daybreak and sunset. So it is in moral and spiritual growth; for law and freedom work together. The law of the harvest, "Whatsoever a man soweth that shall he also reap," is no rigid system of conformity to stereotyped patterns of conduct. One must understand the consequences of selfishness, greed, prejudices, hate, and injustice by personal specific experiences and differentiate between immediate gains and long-time results. One must know by experiences that the positive virtues have superior fruits and understand why specific attitudes and acts do not always bring expected outcomes. It will be far more profitable for a boy or girl to put experiences together, study exceptions to assumed rules, and discover the basic laws of the universe as they actually operate, than to have some parent or teacher keep saying that God does this or that.[2] If the symbol "God" is to be used, it should be reserved for the underlying and integrating phases of life; for otherwise God may be associated with inconsistent and unjust operations. Even if "the rain falleth on the just and the unjust," it may come at a time when it does harm to the just farmer and helps the unjust farmer who has poorer soil.

Appreciation for the abundant resources of nature and for the inexhaustible possibilities in life also requires intelligent and co-operative action to constitute religious response. To pray, "Give us this day our daily bread," might be nothing much more than an attempt to work magic if one failed to understand the ways in which people get bread and the complex processes of production and distribution. Likewise, to say prayers of thanksgiving to God for daily food, or other blessings, may be to ignore the many people and agencies who have contributed to our needs. It is not religious to exalt a vague deity and to discount real people and definite processes. Yet both young people and adults need to realize that underlying, and within, all the operations of people are the forces and resources of nature. This sense of always something more not yet discovered, of creative possibilities of things better than have been found, is a constant inspiration and buoyant feeling stimulating high and sustained efforts. The offset to defeatism when human affairs are depressing is not blind trusts in a "Wholly Other" but intelligent use of resources inherent in co-operative living and in keeping with possibilities of growth and change discoverable in the living universe. Little children, adolescents, and adults, all need repeated experiences in everyday activities of the thrills of creatively solving problems. The range of opportunities runs from guidance of a baby in a home to the settlement of international conflicts.

It is sometimes said that religion is a by-product of large living, and there is a fundamental truth in the statement; for, as growing persons reach out beyond their immediate surroundings and take part in the larger life, meanings, values, and wants change. As they share in the thoughts and actions of others, the interesting possibilities of living unfold; and the consequences of one's behavior are seen in new perspective. It is more religious to act socially because one has found that social action enriches and deepens the meanings and values of life than to pray, "God, help us to love everybody," or "Heavenly Father, bless the hungry children in war-stricken lands." To appreciate the abundant resources of nature and the ways in which there may be plenty for all with good will among all men and to work in that creative process is more religious than to request the big cosmic engineer to keep everyone in mind. Further, it is important in the growth of spiritual attitudes to feel the relative values of this or that particular pleasure, possession, achievement, or point of view. One's present interests should not shut one up in a room without windows and doors. Today had its yesterdays and will have its tomorrows; and, while we make the most we can of today, we need to be big enough to think of yesterday and tomorrow. Everyone's life has its successes and its disappointments, its joys and griefs, its thrills and its chills. To appreciate nature is to take it as it is and to be able to meet what comes with a sense of continuing resource and ability to live worthily. The kindergarten child needs help with his ups and downs—physical, egoistical, social. The adolescent swings to extremes, now on top of the world and now way down under; and he needs the balance of a spiritual perspective. The adult in his more mature thoughtfulness faces endless problems and seeks a hilltop for the larger view.

Throughout the ages poets, artists, philosophers, scientists, historians, preachers, teachers and common men have tried to express their appreciation of the universe. They have done it in many interesting ways; and one important part of religious education is to review some of these products of the past, to evaluate them, and to enrich growing minds with such parts as may be meaningful at different age levels and for varied needs. The range and variety of materials is vast. A few types have been carefully studied, but, gradually, research is opening up new areas and making available rich treasure-houses of religious inspiration. As people go beyond biblical pictures and interpretations into the broad fields of human experience, past and present, perhaps the larger perspective will cause little controversial questions to lose their emotional tensions and permit deeper religious meanings and motivations to emerge.

DISCRIMINATION IN VALUES

When a horse, dog, or other animal is trained, he must obey his master. He is not expected to use his ordinary senses, to discriminate, to be free to satisfy his own desires. Similarly, in military service the majority are expected to accept regimentation, to conform to rules, to submerge their own interests, and to obey.

> Theirs not to reason why,
> Theirs but to do, and die.

Religion has often been presented in like fashion, a matter of conformity, of submission of faith and obedience. It has frequently been said that there are only two ways, the high and the low, the narrow that leads to eternal life and the broad that leads to destruction. The gospel has been one which taught man to surrender his life to Jesus, to trust him, to obey him, to conform to his way, to accept Jesus as Savior and Lord. In this scheme, man must not trust his reason, is not expected to discriminate but, as a good soldier of Jesus Christ, must obey any officer in the army who tells him what is Christ's or God's will. Some people like this kind of religion; for life is too complicated for them. They want a way of escape from its many perplexing problems and an assurance of peace and eternal life. They respond to the conditions of surrender and accept the rules laid down. In some churches the rules are strict, but in others there are a few set requirements with a good bit of lax supervision, and in such a system one does not tend to do more than follow minimum demands. This kind of religion usually stresses mystical experiences as further means of escape from reality. It has been condemned as an opiate, and in many cases it does destroy all tendencies to rational, discriminatory behavior.

In all the better forms of religion, where religion is willing to be tested by its influence on conduct, discrimination is vital; and sacrifice is expected as a means of realizing the highest values and ends of living. The unfortunate thing is that there is little agreement as to what scale of values measures religious development. Theoretically, Christians have taken the standards of the life and teachings of Jesus; but, practically, the interpretations of this Way vary greatly. One group, for instance, quotes Jesus' teachings about self-denial and making one's brother to offend, to prove that Jesus is opposed to drinking alcoholic liquors, while another group is willing to accept the records that he not only drank but provided wine for his friends. When Jesus is taken as authority, one has continual difficulties with other people's interpretations of what Jesus did, would do, or would have his followers do. The general practice is to accept the mores of one's group, to follow whatever customs one finds agreeable, and to rationalize omissions or deviations from the orthodox patterns. Those accustomed to authoritative rules and precepts and to theological or biblical standards do not know how to make true evaluations and discriminations; for they seek to win approval or to avoid disapproval instead of weighing alternatives and formulating principles for choice and action.

In developing discriminatory living, one of the necessary steps is to help children feel the differences in ways of behaving and to cause them to keep these differences in mind as they make their choices and decisions. The spiritual response is quite different from the reaction of an animal which starts to run across the road in front of a moving vehicle and then suddenly turns back because the sign of danger is stronger than the impulse to go ahead. The animal cannot work out principles of safety, and it is useless to try to explain to it the need for looking two ways and for calculating the margins of safety. Human beings have capacities to learn form their own experience and from that of others, and they can profit from educational guidance. A wise parent does not treat a child as a pup but respects his intelligence and stimulates discriminatory thought and actions. As the child grows, he has many decisions to make for which adult guidance is not available and for which it should not be necessary; and it is in such situations that one sees whether early training has been satisfactory. Parents, teachers, and friends serve growing persons best when they stimulate critical judgments, allow them room to experiment and to be independent, and let them see what kind of discriminatory behavior is needed to be trusted.[3]

In the early school grades, teachers call attention to significant differences in qualities of work and conduct and help children to appreciate the superior values. They invite children critically to examine good and bad points and gradually help them to recognize norms that are fair for their grade. As children move ahead in the grades, they find norms and social expectations rising, but there is a perennial problem of motivating them to be self-critical and to put forth their best efforts. There is always a tendency to follow the line of least resistance and to try to get by with as little as possible. Competition, desire for high grades, home pressure, and constant reminders keep some alert, but others either do not feel equal to the expectations or do not find satisfaction in adult standards.

Motivation for discriminatory thought and action is related to growing wants and interests, being dependent upon the strength of particular desires and on general dominating interests. A baby has only two or three major wants; and his preferences are mainly organic, not self-conscious discriminations. The organic factor persists through life, asserting itself in habits and attitudes, but as a person matures, he is capable of objectifying his wants, of perceiving differences in personal and social outcomes, and of making intelligent choices and discriminating acts. Many of his decisions and acts, however, will be made without intellectual differentiation; for emotional tendencies frequently press for release and do not wait for sane judgments. Society is learning gradually to put a premium on conduct that is disciplined, in which differentiations are carefully considered, in which social consequences are taken into account, and in which enduring results have precedence over temporary gains.[4] This is the growth of spiritual values, spiritual sensitivities, with appreciation of how much richer and better life may be when it is controlled by reflective thought and comprehensive objectives.

At every turn, discrimination involves sacrifice; and it is well to examine just what sacrifice means and when it becomes religious. A baby has to learn to unclose his fist and to give up what he holds if he wants something else. It is useless to howl for something which seems important if one is unwilling to sacrifice that which hinders its attainment. A boy in a game has to learn the advantages of team play over selfish and individual acts if he is to get respect from his playmates and be wanted. A businessman needs to find the values in cooperative action which cannot be secured by rugged individualism. Everyone in social relations needs to recognize the benefit that comes from observing the laws of friendship and good will. There is a price for every gain, and what we call sacrifice is but the price for superior and more satisfying ways of living. Physical and material gains cannot be separated from spiritual, but they must be kept subordinate in the mind and purposes of those who would find the highest personal-social values. It is tragic that society frequently gives headline attention to those who have been successful in amassing things, without appraising their worth to the world from which they have taken the loot. But it is easier to see the faults of a Göring bloated with war thefts or of an American war millionaire rich on the profits from other people's sacrifices than it is to appraise the shortcomings of the ordinary citizen who refuses to give time, thought, or resources to the common good.

Too many people are stunted personalities, who have failed to find the joy of social living. They may have begun as spoiled children who were allowed to assert their selfish desires without consideration for the rights and needs of others. But many have never had their imagination really stirred with a vision of the spiritual possibilities of personal-social living and have followed the only interests which home, school, church, or society has awakened. Everything that is being done by individuals and organizations to enlist people in community enterprises, social service, and cultural advancement is a wholesome counteraction to prevailing selfish tendencies. But in promoting these causes one sometimes finds a failure to trust in the appeal of spiritual values or an inability to make such values meaningful and attractive. Low motives are appealed to, such as buying war bonds to get a good interest and later to have a chance to buy luxuries, giving to avoid paying taxes to the government, seeking status in the community by gifts or service, matching what others are doing, and even saving one's conscience from feelings of guilt for the sufferings from war. To make sacrifices spiritual they must have relation to increase in human values, to the furtherance of conditions affording larger freedom and privilege to other people.

All through this study of discrimination the writer has felt the paucity of ideas in most people and the thinness of culture. One of the war censors has spoken of the absence of significant ideas in most of the mail that he had to read. Even in a great world crisis, the common man was unable, or unwilling, to share great constructive thoughts. But he was not much worse than those in places of governmental responsibility who had no philosophy or plans to deal with defeated enemies. Most people drift along, letting things happen, without large purposes and expanding philosophies to guide them. It is impossible to be discriminating if one does not have ideas and dominating desires, and those must be continually growing. It seems as if most of our education, general and religious, fails to stimulate the imagination. People get words but fail to understand the full meanings of the ideas which they are supposed to convey. Most seem to be moving around in a fog, without any clear sense of direction and with only blurred concepts of what is going on.

To be discriminating, one must want to go somewhere, do something, become something that is definite and worth while. One must see alternatives clearly, feel that it makes a great difference for one's self and for others what decisions one makes, and have some faith and skills to undertake significant living. In some homes ideas seem to be going in and coming out like bees in a hive, and there is never a lack of interesting things to talk over, while in other homes people seem more like cattle. In some classes in school, teachers have pupils working overtime to get data to enrich discussions, and youngsters have ideas. In some churches preachers have ideas in their sermons, and people expect to be stirred to thought and definite convictions. There are always a few people in every community who have an interest in social issues, new ideas, and possible changes in economics, politics, religion, science, and other human affairs. But many have not much more than a recent headline from a newspaper, or a vague idea of what somebody said, on anything that is of outstanding importance for human welfare. Instead of religious education being largely a matter of listening to sermons without saying a word, listening to church-school teachers without any responsibility for getting facts on vital topics, we need more home gatherings, community groups, school panels, church forums, and conferences of representatives of various human interests, where current problems and basic ideas are threshed out regularly by serious-minded people. Spiritual insight does not come by mere intuition but by intensive, discriminating thinking. And radical changes are not achieved by impulsive fanatics but by people who are willing to pay the price for slow educational work and carefully planned programs of action.

One final principle that must be emphasized in dealing with these spiritual growth factors is the influence of group attitudes upon individuals. A child reflects his home in indifference, prejudice, or fair-mindedness. Youth follow the fashion of a gang, and adults are Republicans, Methodists, Catholics, or whatever it may be that they have inherited. There is usually very little discrimination in a group, and it may be difficult to tell what determines its patterns of behavior, but when one belongs, one does as others do and says what others say. There are groups, as we have pointed out, which are primarily planned to stimulate critical thought and actions but this is not true of most homes, schools, churches, clubs, political organizations, social gatherings, trade meetings, and the like. In an ordinary group if an individual introduces a new idea, he is put on the defense at once, and if it is unconvincingly stated, he is the butt of ridicule. Instead of creating an atmosphere favorable to critical, constructive thought, in which each member seeks to help the other to express his ideas and to find rational grounds for policies and programs, the tendency is for most to keep silent while some self-confident individual tells the others what is to be said and done. Young people have so much desire to be with those of their own age that they put up with almost any kind of group in order to satisfy the gregarious urge. If a keen mind finds a chum or a small coterie with whom he can share ideas and do things that seem worth while, he is fortunate; for many such have to live as lone wolves. Everyone needs to belong to a number of groups which are stimulating and which give one incentive to think and to act with daring freedom.

The average adolescent in a cultured community who belongs to neighborhood, school, or club groups is not likely to swing far from the average standards of the community. He is not likely, however, to be particularly discriminating or refined in matters of dress, sex attitudes, personal habits, or ordinary interests, at least above the usual habits of the group. What is needed for most youth seems to be a variety of activities so that they are not controlled by one pattern or gang. There are good possibilities in home gatherings, school clubs and parties, athletic teams, community centers, teen-age organizations with national direction and promotion, discussion groups, church organizations, hobby groups, and other local activities. The young people should feel responsibility for programs and general policies, but some wise adults acceptable with young people are needed in the background. They should be encouraged to plan regular and special times for discussions of current topics, personal problems, religious issues, service projects, and whatever they as young citizens should be interested in. They can as they grow older, and especially when they leave school, take a part in general community gatherings, co-operative societies, nonpartisan political meetings, conferences and study groups, and other movements in this country dealing with human needs and welfare—health clinics, intercultural educational projects, organizations for interracial understanding, movements for research and economic reform, interfaith organizations, service agencies for special needs, and hundreds of other types. Religious education must teach people to evaluate these, to give discriminating support, and to keep spiritual values to the fore. There are many outlets for those who seek a higher level of life, but there are dangers in emotional drives which are not tempered with keen intellectual understanding of issues and strategies. Many start enthusiastically with high hopes but find their efforts futile because of poorly planned or inadequatey supported procedures. Discrimination and sacrifice are the conditions of progress, and spirituality which lacks these tends to be a formal gesture.

Chapter Five

Responsibility and Co-operation

THIS chapter deals with responsibility and accountability as a twin pair of essential qualities in religion and with co-operative fellowship both as a complement to the individualistic sense of worth and as an expansion of social sensitivity. The intermeshing of these various factors is the picture life presents, a complex in which the different spiritual qualities appear as prismatic colors.

RESPONSIBILITY AND ACCOUNTABILITY

Responsibility and accountability are the conditions essential to freedom, and freedom is the *sine qua non* of spiritual growth. Man is so made that he must act both independently and dependently, a member of a closely interrelated society of persons. In his early years, society continually reminds the individual that he is dependent and accountable, but, as he matures, it expects him to show independence and self-responsibility. While the two are inseparable all through life, most people would be better if they learned to be independent earlier and maintained a sense of dependence and accountability in later years; for even though no one has the right to do as he pleases without respect to the rights, needs, and wants of others, it is also true that one is quite mature before he is able to keep a fair balance in social obligations. Religion has built up principles and rules to indicate man's responsibilities, and in some cults the duties of worship, offerings, obedience to prescribed rules, and loyalties are set forth in detail. The difficulty is that interpretations of duties in one period of history, built around certain theological points of view, are carried forward into a later period where they are only abitrary remnants of an old order, having no meaningful justification. As this is being written, a radio evangelist is trying to impress his audience with their duty to tithe, but his arguments are quite different from the ancient Hebrew teachings and still more different from the obligations which a liberal minister would use for support of a religious cause. Emphases upon immersion, preparation for the Second Coming, and hundreds of other doctrines which once were obligations upon a Christian because of interpretations of Jesus' commands are now shifting to entirely different teachings and new interpretations. Instead of taking the text, "Ye are not your own for ye are bought with a price," as a literal bargain with God which left one under certain compulsions, the tendency is to give it a broad, general turn, recalling the fact that we are the product of endless sacrifices and have an obligation to serve humanity. Some modernists recoil so strongly from old slogans which revivalists used, such as "Get right with God"; "Prepare to meet thy God"; "The day of the Lord is at hand"; and "Fear him who is able to destroy both soul and body in hell", that they fail to see that these people lived in a very different world, though they had a sense of accountability which people today do not have.

Today we have more privileges than people of the past, but we should not take them for granted, to use as we please. Perhaps the meaning and possibilities of freedom are modern concepts, but it must not be forgotten that what we enjoy is the result of the unselfish struggles of many of our predecessors. Two world wars remind us of the dangers that threaten freedom and of the terrible cost of preserving it. The hope is that now a larger portion of the world may share its privileges; but they will not, unless these spiritual qualities of responsibility and accountability become working principles in a new world order. Likewise, change in a hundred other social issues waits on the growth of this spirit—relations of labor and management, domestic relations and less divorce, equable distribution of economic goods, race relations, correction of alcoholic habits, higher standards in public office, and all such situations where indifference on the part of the privileged groups permits evils to multiply. Each one is his brother's keeper, and the religious spirit is shown as each gives more time and thought to the solution of human ills. In this section we show how this spirit may grow.

There are many signs of a growing appreciation of freedom and a recognition of the obligations necessary to keep it operative in this and other lands. It is getting its foundations in better home training. The injunction, "Children, obey your parents," is being supplemented by the teaching to parents, "Parents, respect your children." A father was rebuked by his three-year-old for not being dependable when the youngster answered, "Daddy, I can be trusted, but you don't trust me." The boy needed more freedom instead of more restrictions. One is continually surprised on the playground, in school, and in many community relationships, to see how dependable, honest, and trustworthy children and young people are when given responsibilities and a reasonable amount of freedom. A first-grade teacher left her room for a few minutes, to find on her return that there was quite a commotion. She saw only the smallest boy out of his seat when she entered, and he was running around the room. As she was about to punish him, three older boys said that it was not fair to punish the little fellow when they were more to blame than he was. The teacher talked over the values of being orderly when she was absent and asked whether they thought they could manage better again. They responded well. In many high schools student government is helping to develop morale and to permit larger measures of freedom than once were thought possible.

Only a small fraction of society is criminal, or even delinquent to a degree requiring official action. The vast majority observe the laws and have a sense of social responsibility. While we lament the fact that there are so many horrible crimes and that our newspapers are full of stories of theft, murder, rape, and cruelties, these are failures of only a few people among the millions of decent, self-respecting citizens. In school athletics and clubs young people have shown excellent capacities for responsible actions, as is witnessed by Scout leaders, 4-H Club directors, and Y.M.C.A. and Y.W.C.A. secretaries. In labor circles there is an increasing sense of responsibility and a feeling for both consumers' and management's needs and rights. In government some of the finest examples of unselfish service have been shown, responsibility not merely to a constituency but also to the country at large and to humanity in international relationships. All such responses are reasons for religious leaders moving outside church programs to stimulate and to further in as many ways as possible these manifestations of growing spiritual values. We need to look at the positive facts of evolving righteousness if we are to have faith in a righteous cause.

Every sign of advance increases the desire for more, for the religious spirit is dynamic, always seeking flying goals. This is different from a pessimistic wail about sin, which some seem to think marks a religious devotee. Progress is not made by keeping one's eyes on one's failures but by conserving every gain and humbly, though vigorously, pursuing possible achievements. In doing this, one must have confidence in one's judgments and a sense of aggressive responsibility. Religion is more than conformity to other people's standards, trying to please someone, and seeking to meet the pressure that is being put on one by associates. Parents who want children to become free persons who can exercise their own minds and decide what is right and wrong must give them opportunities to test out their own ideas and let them weigh the parental advice. Teachers who are preparing pupils for responsibilities in a democratic order must give them problems to solve and must cultivate creative, energetic spirits. In the church dogmatic statements as to God's will and demands must give place to teaching which places responsibility upon people to choose among the possible alternatives in a flexible world order. Ideas of absoluteness in divine prerogatives ignore the freedom essential for development of self-respecting personalities. The mistakes and failures of life are inevitable in the learning process; man is not to be branded as a hopeless sinner waiting for divine deliverance. He must learn by experience or surrender his significance as a responsible agent in a developing universe. Religious education should identify the kinds of situations in which responsibility can be given at each level and in the varied relations of social living and should develop expectations for effective and faithful fulfilment.

The question of discipline arises as soon as one proposes more freedom, for one must be realistic. What can be done with those who are slow to learn or who refuse to be social? On an international scale society has so far seen only one way, and that is war, to kill off enough people to make the rest want peace and to seek working bases for friendly relations. War is being subjected to severe criticism, while the United Nations seek terms of enduring peace.

Today, education is committed to more democratic methods, and parents are recognizing that the old adage "Spare the rod and spoil the child" is a relic of a primitive culture. Society is trying to handle delinquents and criminals by more humane, constructive methods. The old penal system did not change human nature, for reformatories and prisons were but breeding places for more crime. The problems of discipline are spiritual problems wherever found and involve religious education, though not necessarily theological education. One does not have to talk of God to cause a person to see that freedom implies responsibility and that we all have inescapable obligations to others. Appreciation for the universal law must grow out of multiplied experiences of specific adjustments which prove its meaning and worth. Theologians may try to work in a field of generalized abstractions, but the religious educator cannot. He begins with the specific, encourages as much generalization as his particular group is ready for, and then goes back to the specific to test meanings and to develop motivations.

A constant problem in trying to make responsibility and accountability attractive is the fact that it is impossible to keep a balanced and just situation. To ask children to respect their parents and others when they are not fairly respected themselves is futile. To ask young people of the lower, or middle, economic class to practice economy as a social duty, when they see waste and extravagance among the more privileged, is irritating. Many citizens rebel against unfair taxes and avoid what they can, because they see public money spent without regard to reasonable accountability. Even in church organizations one sees abuse of power and trust. While we must always work in an imperfect social order and while responsibility must be placed on individuals to help improve the situation instead of perpetuating unsatisfactory conditions, the process of religious education must stress mutual obligations. We shall always need pioneers, leaders willing to set a pace, heroes of the commonplace, and religion should make their roles inspiring and challenging. But at the same time we need to analyze socioeconomic problems, conflicts of interests and responsibilities, and methods of rectifying wrongs, indicating specific changes desirable by all parties concerned. Even when this understanding is made plain, somebody must start the good work. A parent, teacher, or public leader must set the example of sincere, intelligent effort to be fair and responsible in meeting obligations; and strong organizations and nations must do likewise.

Conscience has been the name given to responsible, conscientious behavior, but it has been treated in religious circles as a special divine gift rather than a product of social experience. It has been defined as "the voice of God in the soul of man," which is good poetry but is not psychologically or pedagogically clear. The critic asks, How does one know what is the voice of God? and, What part of a living, growing personality is the soul of man? If hearing the voice of God is growing appreciation for that which works for the greatest common good, it should not be taught as something vague and mystical. If the soul of man is his growing sensitivity to the highest meanings and values of life, it should be recognized as the cumulative product of many specific adjustments, all of which are subject to educational direction and guidance. Conscience is shown in specific attitudes and acts. It grows as one practices visualizing desirable social situations, personal behavior patterns, and ways of realizing them. Conscience is an inner readiness developed by satisfying experiences and experimental living. It will be cultivated differently at each age level and in varied situations. Religious education needs a much richer body of illustrations of exemplary behavior from ongoing life and less dependence upon exceptional classical pictures. Conscience must be more than an unpleasant feeling of duty and more than a sense of smugness in doing things others neglect. It should be a feeling of growing into intelligent appreciation of the lines of progress, of being in tune with the best that life holds.

An individual's sense of duty always involves the feeling of belonging to a group or groups which have obligations. Families have duties to neighboring families and to the community at large, duties relative to keeping physical property respectable and attractive, to giving children social training and sharing responsibility for supervision of them outside the home, and to maintaining community resources and standards at as high a level as possible. In good schools a community spirit grows which is passed on from year to year and which gives pupils pride in their school and feelings of responsibility for living up to expectations.[1] During the war citizens were continually reminded of duties to the state, obligations to those who served them in the military forces, and needs for keeping up quotas. We need peacetime obligations which are defined as definitely and presented with methods as urgent and compelling as wartime developed. Churches have always stressed church responsibilities, denominational obligations, and, to some degree, what a united religious front must mean and do. All appeals for loyal support have been colored by specific pictures of human need and have been successful as emotions have been stirred.

In view of the multiplying agencies set up for service to humanity there is need for critical study of respective values in different organizations in order that responsibility may not be dulled by a sense of inability to share in more than a few of the many important causes. Churches should justify their programs and claims in the same clear way as a civil liberties association or as a committee to help refugees or children in some foreign land. It is no more religious to pay a subscription to a church than to take a share in the budget of a reform or social service organization. One may meet spiritual obligations as a parent, a taxpayer, an honest businessman, a member of a humanitarian organization, or as a good neighbor. Religious education can well afford to evaluate group responsibilities and opportunities and to interest growing persons in them, as needed agencies in building a spiritual world.

One other factor should be dealt with before leaving this section: the frequent experience of guilt when one has failed to meet one's obligations and particularly when such failure has meant suffering or harm to another. Some religious leaders seem to have a malicious delight in developing feelings of guilt because they think that they can offer a forgiveness and a deliverance that will bring a compensating sense of relief and joy. Their supernatural religious medicine does not always work, and sometimes feelings of guilt drive people insane. While we are trying to develop responsible persons, we must not make the religious way impossible, or even impossible without supernatural help; for responsibility implies capacity to meet obligations. Everyone, as long as he lives, will be making mistakes and injuring others, but neither indifference or depressing guiltiness will improve the situation. There is no way of cleaning the slate either by the magic of a priest's absolution or by accepting a Protestant theological formula about Christ's atonement. To express verbal regret and to receive verbal forgiveness may help an adjustment, but improved attitudes and actions demonstrate sincerity and possible expectations for the future. When a sense of guilt is more than a spur to reflection and maximum effort, it is harmful, and may produce a psychopathic condition. There is no value in magnifying a sense of guilt, once a wrong is recognized and desire to change is sincerely manifest. This is true for an adolescent, a seasoned criminal, or a warring nation. The religious attitude for the offender is more than humility and confession of guilt, and the wronged must do more than express willingness to forgive. Both need to improve things in the light of lessons learned, and there is usually plenty for each party to do to make the better way practical and desirable. Religious education has spent too much time in trying to vindicate an offender before a hypothetical heavenly court and has not dealt with the necessary adjustments to give the divine process favorable conditions for new growth. Sometimes a psychiatrist is needed and sometimes merely a faithful friend. Each case is different, and religious education must learn to do case work instead of depending upon a gospel broadcast. Wounds are sometimes deep and hard to heal.

CO-OPERATIVE FELLOWSHIP

In this area of co-operative fellowship we discuss the possibilities of raising the level of spiritual living by giving attention to the character of the groups to which people belong. One of the peculiarities of human beings is their tendency to organize into groups; and, as civilization grows, variety multiplies. Most of what people think and do is affected by their membership in groups. Sociology has helped us to see that individuals are units in organized society, each a socius of the socii, and in studying them one must not treat them as if they were isolated. Religion deals both with the individual and with society, but sometimes the interrelationship has been forgotten. Jesus suggested the intimate association of the two when he said, "The kingdom of God is within you."

Under social sensitivity we considered the relation between individuals, and, of course, this sensitivity is at the root of all fellowship; but the combination of elements in co-operative fellowship is quite different from that in social sensitivity. The character of a fellowship is twofold: (1) a creative interaction among the members and (2) sustaining strength and combined power, both of which are greater and different from what might be expected in the summation of the individual resources. The unique and important nature of this co-operative fellowship is emphasized by a statement of an outstanding scientist after research upon plant structures, animals, and humans. He said, "For the higher levels of living we need the cooperative inter-relationship of widely differentiated units."[2] That is, in the evolution of all forms of life there is a constant differentiation in function of various organized parts, but for the most efficient living there must be continual co-operation among the parts, none being isolated.

In modern society there are thousands of different social groupings involving every kind of function, but all are interdependent; and the same person may belong to many organizations. For instance, when a baby is born, he is, by virtue of being a person, a member of a family, a neighborhood, a community, a state, a nation, and a world organization. He may also be enrolled in a church, a clinic, a bank, and even registered for a special college. How far he may become an active member and share the co-operative fellowship of these and other groups depends upon his growth and upon ever changing physical and social factors. In several city high schools the writer found scores of extra-curricular organizations, and in some communities adolescents are subject to a regular barrage of appeals to belong to groups for dancing, card-playing, athletics, music, art projects, dramatics, camping, discussions, relief work or social service, special hobby interests, and other short-term or long-period projects. Adults, likewise, have opportunities and responsibilities in an endless variety of organized activities. The theory underlying our functional religious approach is that all these have possibilities of positive or negative spiritual influence and that we should cease thinking of religious education as being primarily a church function. To the degree that any co-operative fellowship lifts life above the animal and mechanistic level, gives it significance in a universal scheme of growing values, stirs purposes toward maximum fulfilment, and fortifies spiritual outreach of any kind such as we are describing in this functional analysis, the ends of religion are being attained.[3]

The simplest form of co-operative fellowship is in the intimate relations of two people—close friends, husband and wife, partners in business, associates in a critical undertaking, mutually dependent fellow-sufferers, advocates of a common cause. As others are included in any grouping, the possibilities of free and intimate exchange of ideas, sharing of interests, and full agreement as to ends and means are reduced, with a consequent difference in outcomes. Yet from an educational point of view there is no limit to the improvement of conditions furthering co-operative fellowship. This is being realized even on an international scale today. The leaders of different nations may and do get together for face-to-face conversations and mutual understandings. They communicate with each other by telephone, wireless, intermediaries who travel by fast planes, and by the constant radio broadcasts of events and their interpretation. Conferences are held on every sort of topic; public discussion of common and conflicting interests takes place on the radio, in forums, and in published writings. Concerted efforts are made to gain fellowship and co-operation relative to matters of critical concern to each and all. Prejudices and selfish interests are analyzed and subjected to frank criticism. Let us, then, review a few of the ways in which this spiritual quality emerges and may be developed in a comprehensive program of religious education.

Since the family has long been regarded as the basic social group, it is encouraging to find how much attention is being given to preparation for marriage and family life. While statistics and daily papers reveal the large percentage of divorces and wrecked homes, it is probably true that the level of family living is steadily rising in all its major values. It is easy to glorify a past ideal, but the fact is that many homes in the past were very barren in aesthetic, social, and spiritual qualities; and many, held together by economic necessity or by social pressure, might better have been disbanded. In churches, schools, and other community agencies there is considerable teaching and counseling relative to courtship, sex relations, homemaking, care of children, financing and budgeting, and special problems. The meaning and possible development of co-operative fellowship between husband and wife, with children, with friends, and with people representing many different interests are being made specific, practical, and attractive. The democratic spirit, creative interaction of minds, and sense of purposeful living are being stimulated and refined in all relationships, with possibilities far greater and more lasting than any which depended upon a formal family worship. The latter may be transformed and become a vital integrating factor, but it never can be a substitute for the delicate adjustments of daily living.[4]

Next to family life, probably the most important kind of experience is that of friendship. An educated, cultured, well-to-do city dweller recently confided to another person, "I have no friends, no persons with whom I have real fellowship." He is undoubtedly typical of a good many other lonely souls. They have many acquaintances and associates, but they have never taken time, or found occasion, for cultivating friends who could share things with them and with whom they could have deeply satisfying experiences. Beginning in early childhood everyone needs friends, those of one's own age and immediate circle and others of different backgrounds with whom one can have mutual bonds. The art of making and keeping friends is something which can be learned; but few give enough time, thought, or unselfish effort to achieving its finest forms. Little children need help in understanding one another, in finding things they can do together with satisfaction and ways by which they may serve each other. Adolescents need more than a corner drugstore in which to cultivate friendships. Young people and adults cannot be limited to denominational lines. Plans for stimulating and maturing friendships need community co-operation, consideration of varied group activities, and improvement of conditions for freest and fullest growth of co-operating friendliness.

While the church has been frequently rated as the ideal group for co-operative fellowship, it has functioned only in limited directions and has not drawn unto itself as many people as it should who want this type of experience. Its sectarian character and its tendency to follow a few stereotyped practices have prevented it from serving the varied needs of people which modern community life presents. Yet it is true that churches have functioned in many communities and in many periods of history as the major rallying points for spiritual values. Today the best contributions to co-operative fellowship by the church are its discussion groups, conferences, camps, and informal meetings. There is no opportunity for creative interaction in the formal services and, in large churches, no expectation of fellowship beyond friendly gestures in the Sunday morning service. In most city churches young people have fewer intimate friends than in school. That is unfortunate, for a good liberal church should offer young people occasion for fellowship at its highest level. While some will maintain that worship is the unique place for fellowship with God and with one's fellow-man, many will discount this mysticism and find more real satisfaction in a critical study of social issues, cosmic resources, and co-operative possibilities for world reconstruction. It is possible to have strong emotional loyalties centered around blind beliefs because of dynamic leaders, but a stronger and more far-reaching fellowship must rest on intelligent convictions and on large human interests.

The public school offers children and young people more opportunities for co-operative thinking and acting than any other organization, and modern education is seeking to make the most possible out of such situations during these formative years. It democratically binds people together without respect for class, creed, race, or nationality difference. Beginning in the nursery school, with carefully selected equipment, a child may play by himself, or with others, as he feels inclined and able socially. He is not forced to co-operate with others, but, if he wants a wagon, slide, or other apparatus which the rest must share, he has to learn the rules for co-operative play and abide by them. He soon finds the shared fun more stimulating and satisfying and accepts the rules, learning by experience that they have real value in necessary adjustments. In the kindergarten, children talk freely with one another, invite each other to see what they are doing, work on small committees, formulate rules for themselves, find special friends, and generally move forward in co-operative fellowship. From here on up through the grades they find an increasing variety of group experiences—committees and project groups, matched teams in athletics and recreation, class activities, and school assemblies. While many events in the classroom and on the playground are competitive, skilful teachers help the children to enjoy a fellowship that transcends the divisiveness of competition. They learn to be good sports, to be interested in fair play, to consider the rights and fun of their opponents, and to be able to take a gain or loss in equally good spirit.

In the high school, groups have more complex activities, standards are higher, more self-discipline is expected, and the resulting fellowship is more meaningful. In some schools cliques are formed in which the fellowship is narrow and exclusive, but under good supervision these are reduced to a minimum, and other more favorable groupings are encouraged. Everyone wants to belong to a significant group, but groups should not be too large if each person is to have a responsible part in a co-operative undertaking. Variety is expected, but there are always a few favorite organizations, and some clubs have to split up into several sections. In some groups individual hobbies are developed; in others community projects are launched; and, in the majority, school subjects such as science, history, civics, art, or a language are the bases of informal investigations and discussions. As the kinds of experiences in these different groups vary so greatly, the administration finds it desirable from an educational point of view to watch individual choices and to give counsel for broad development.[5]

At the college and university level the problems of providing healthy, stimulating experiences of this kind of co-operative fellowship center around dormitory life, fraternities and sororities, athletic teams, drama groups, school papers, dances, parties, and the rest of the ordinary and extraordinary groupings found on a campus. Administrators try to steer programs, but most students want a large measure of freedom. Influences aimed at lifting interests and goals to as high a level as possible have to be indirect, for students must discover things for themselves and take definite responsibilities. They will be expected to use freedom wisely when they graduate, and they must learn to value it and to use it with discretion in college. Different church organizations, and the Y.M.C.A. and Y.W.C.A., have tried to introduce special programs and organized groups into schools and colleges, with the assumption in many cases that they are offering the only religious opportunities in these institutions. They may have attractive and worth-while programs, but they seldom reach more than a fraction of the young people and the concept of religion tends to be theological and biblical rather than functional. It may be of some value to talk of good and God, but evil and man require careful attention, and on a campus good and evil are very specific. Perhaps the greatest evil is the lack of significant goals and the failure of co-operative fellowship in the classroom or informal group to stir vision or purpose.

Another important field for development of spiritual values is in the co-operative fellowship growing in the labor union movements. Organized religion and labor are meeting more frequently and on terms of mutual respect, but the most fertile soil for growth of these functional qualities of religion is in the educational committees, the policy-making committees, the political action committees, and the regular meetings of district and local unions. One cannot study the history of the labor movement over the last one hundred years without appreciating the marvelous rise in standards of living, sense of worth and power, and assertion of rights, of the common man. Working through his union, he has developed a fine degree of co-operative fellowship, locally, nationally, and internationally. The majority of the leaders seem to be high-minded, unselfish, and committed to the welfare of the common man. Because the interests of the common man and those of the privileged classes often conflict, it is not always possible for the latter to appreciate the gains of the former, so that the faults of organized labor stand out more prominently than its virtues. The faults and shortcomings of organized labor are many, and its leaders are not unconscious of them, but unions are making slow headway and would make much faster progress if they did not have to fight intrenched interests for every inch they gain.

The programs of many union groups are amazing, including wholesome recreation, social service, citizenship training, general education, personal counseling, community projects, study of national and international questions affecting human welfare, and many other things, depending upon personnel and local conditions. Some of labor's leaders are men trained for the ministry who have given themselves to this work with as deep a sense of mission as any churchman. More leaders are coming from college graduates who have a vision of a new day and a feeling of the power in organized labor which needs intelligent direction. Through its journals and other publications, through the conferences in which its leaders continually engage, over the radio, and by ceaseless personal contacts, the ideals and working goals of the common man are being voiced and pursued. Religious education must be comprehensive enough to include this area of human advance.

Again, in considering the agencies and movements which further co-operative fellowship, one needs to evaluate the purposes, programs, and general spirit of such groups as Scouting, 4-H clubs, Red Cross, voters' leagues, educational associations, tolerance and antidiscrimination movements, relief agencies, health centers, service clubs, medical service and hospitalization plans, housing projects, and the thousand and one types of organizations directed toward human betterment. In these varied groups people are meeting regularly, giving unselfishly of time, money, and talents to make life more livable for others and to inspire others to work with them for higher ideals. These agencies offer excellent outlets for religious desires, and the faith, hope, and love manifest in many of these organizations are fine illustrations of religion in action. They provide the kind of situation in which emotions do not grow cold, and idealism does not evaporate in discussion. They need to be carefully evaluated, continually revised as to specific goals and methods, and directed by persons of keen intellect as well as warm devotion.

Lastly in this analysis of situations favoring growth of co-operative fellowship is the field of recreation. There are many types of leisure-time activity which give opportunity for creative co-operative expression. Drama and music are two mediums in which fine forms of good fellowship are achieved. A group of children may be transformed by an informal play in which they act out a vivid scene and bring it to a satisfying conclusion. The more careful preparation of dramatizations by an older group, using well-chosen subjects, affords occasions for thought on typical human problems and development of refined social attitudes. Festivals of song and instrumental music, enriched by pageantry, give other opportunities for use of talents and expression of group ideals. It is interesting that one of the oldest and most common habits of people is to provide a meal and some relaxing entertainment when matters of serious import are to be considered by a group who are meeting together for the first time. The spirit of fellowship is furthered both by friendly social contacts and by the necessity of facing important responsibilities together, but the need of friendliness is stressed in the setting. Even international leaders find this good technique and do not depend upon rational judgments alone to effect co-operation. All forms of recreation—athletics, dancing, movie attendance, travel, camping, hobbies, reading, arts and handicraft, social clubs, dining and chatting, informal games, discussions, and other social activities—may contribute positive or negative factors to the spiritual growth of those who participate and may be discriminatingly selected for fullest life enrichment.

General education has felt the need for developing good taste, skills, and variety of interests with reference to leisure-time activities and is doing some important things toward this end, both for young people during their schooling and in the use of the school as a community center. Churches have tended to follow the line of least resistance, giving little guidance in evaluation or creative change, while delivering restrictive exhortations upon debasing forms. When drinking, gambling, dancing, smoking, or other practices are made taboo, there are seldom any clear factual data or convincing principles presented on the basis of which intelligent action might be taken, and the custom of one's group tends to be accepted. Whether or not these are harmful and whether or not they involve the question of sacrificing a lesser value for a greater are not dealt with as they need to be from the standpoint of religious education. Most social customs need refinement if they are to contribute to the best forms of co-operative fellowship and personality development. The unfortunate thing is that many people let down their standards in a large part of their recreation, accepting things as they are instead of working for their improvement. If commercial institutions are to raise the quality of their recreational offerings, they must be stimulated and supported by church, school, and other community and national groups. Functional religion admits that its quality and power are tested by the degree to which the behavior of people in their free time, and in social fellowship, is controlled by their spiritual ideals.[6]

Chapter Six

Quest and Integration

THE two types of experience with which we are concerned in this chapter, quest for truth and realization of values, and integration of experiences into a working philosophy of life, are good indices of the vitality of religion. As long as organized religion welcomes questions and does not hesitate to relate its beliefs and attitudes to the findings of science, history, and philosophy, it may expect to have a respectable and influential position in world thought. To the degree that it tends to remove its teachings and practices from free critical study, claiming for them special revelation, assuming a special means of appreciation, and keeping its treasures as particularly sacred, it cannot expect to be regarded as anything more than an esoteric interest. Further, as long as proponents of different world faiths or of sectarian doctrines refuse to subject their presuppositions and traditions to critical-historical study, demonstrating their fearless search for truth, we cannot look forward to organized religion being a radical transforming power in the world. Instead of vague general phrases which may be manipulated into any number of different shapes without losing any of their vagueness, we need specific concrete experiences which may be evaluated and working beliefs which may be refined and re-stated as growth in meanings warrant. In general, we may say that the attitudes expressed in these two categories are those of buoyant faith in the growing insights into the meanings and possibilities of abundant life for all and of confident trust in the pervasive transforming qualities of basic religious ideas and values. We believe that the inquiring mind with its capacity for discriminating appreciation is the chief organ of religious sensitivity and that the totality of experience is a firmer base for religious faith than any isolated segment. With this point of view we proceed with an analysis of ways in which the above-named religious factors may be expected to grow.

QUEST FOR TRUTH AND REALIZATION OF VALUES

A healthy, growing child asks questions as soon as he can talk, and the more he learns the more he is likely to keep on asking questions. The normal reaction is for this spirit of inquiry to continue with increasing sense of the complexity but solvability of most problems, unless parents, teachers, or others repress and discourage this search for knowledge. School offers children opportunities to explore both present objects and processes and the learnings of the centuries. They discover change, growth, laws, and interesting possibilities of development, all of which give meaning and motivation toward fuller living. They learn to analyze problems and social issues into their component factors, to weigh their relative significance, and to formulate conclusions as to causes and effects. They learn to think with others, to exchange ideas, to understand reasons for different opinions, to use their own judgments, and to test the consequences of different plans. While modern education tends to put its emphasis upon learning to think critically and creatively, it recognizes the need for a body of knowledge.[1] One cannot think without ideas, and it is foolish to discount the findings of men through the ages. Appreciation for the learnings of the past is, however, dependent upon each individual's own rich experience and active imagination. The learnings of others cannot be transmitted without the mental and emotional response of interested persons. The educational method must therefore start from where an individual is and bring in experience of the race when interest in what others have thought and done is awakened. Sometimes education seems to give so much attention to the importance of each generation becoming familiar with the best ideas, attitudes, and methods of the past that it seems to ignore the psychological preparation necessary to make this meaningful and interesting. Learning does not begin with the past but with the present which the past has given us.

One illustration of the difficulty of using historical data and the need for critical creative thought when dealing with past records is shown in a sixth-grade unit on the history of Chicago. The children of a Chicago school were stimulated to see the possible value and fun in writing up the story of their city. The teacher made some records available; visits were made to several institutions where exhibits of historical materials were on display; newspapers and other records were examined; and a number of people were interviewed. The children found that they could get a fairly good outline of the history from the days of Indian settlements down to the present but that there were many details about which there were confusing and conflicting records. They tried to explain some of these contradictory accounts, and by comparing ideas and impressions they worked out together a fairly satisfactory story. The experience in this project was found useful in many later situations as they tried to reconstruct historical happenings and to interpret different points of view. It is the kind of mental discipline on specific, concrete material needed for examination of historical religious records and for constant differentiation between facts and interpretation of facts.

The religious educator turns repeatedly to the general educator who has the pupils five day a week to see what he is doing and what young people are learning. He finds him beset by different theorists, the classicists who emphasize historical content, the functionalists and experimentalists who want studies centered in the present world of experience, and the vocationalists who think of the practical tasks of making a living. All of these points of view have important elements for a well-educated person, and they should be organized into a balanced program. The two most pressing concerns are whether growing persons are being taught to think critically and creatively and whether they have an interest in using their own experience and skills, as well as general human experience, in the solution of personal-social problems. While it is valuable in a democracy for everyone to have a common body of ideas, values, and general attitudes, it is also desirable that a wide range of specialized knowledge and skills be developed. Each individual should find opportunities in several areas of life for cultivation and release of his potentialities, and these should be integrated into a wholesome philosophy and purpose in living. He should see rich possibilities in his daily vocation, in his relationships as a citizen, in his family life, in his church and other organizational relations, and in general cultural interests. To all these, general education may make significant contributions at all age levels, and religious education is in part the spirit, attitudes, and values being stimulated in the whole process. The writer does not agree with those who would separate spiritual ends of the public school from those of the church and organized religion. The trend toward naturalism would do away with this unfortunate dualism and would unify life around great beliefs and purposes.

One trend in education which deserves special attention at this point is the tendency to short-cut the process of learning by a system of indoctrination. Certain ends are assumed to be so important that educators want them assured and attained without delay. For instance, democracy is taken as an ideal to be transmitted, and a set of techniques and verbalisms are organized to make it the accepted way of life. In order to secure a democracy, totalitarian methods are used; and the rights and needs of freedom of thought and judgment are ignored. If democracy is a desirable end, it will not be lost in a critical, creative process of education in which the perspective of history and analysis of alternatives are carefully considered. Vital democracy is not conformity to a set pattern of ideas or practices but rather free co-operative thinking and experimenting. There is yet much to

be done to develop capacities and attitudes equal to the radical logic
of democracy, and it will not be attained by merely talking emotionally about the ideals. Indoctrination is a reversion to the outgrown idea of education by direct transmission. It may be the tool of
a totalitarian regime where obedient puppets are wanted, but it does
not develop spiritual responses consonant with democratic ideals.[2]

Recognizing, then, the essential spiritual qualities in good general
education, what are the special problems of the religious quest, if
there are any special ones not to be included in general education?
The majority of people brought up in conventional religion would
state the central topics for religious education as outlined in the seven
objectives of the International Council of Religious Education:[3] fos-
tering a consciousness of God, experiencing Jesus Christ as Savior
and Lord, interpreting the universe as a Christian, appreciating the
Bible, being loyal to the church, developing a Christian social order,
and attaining a Christlike character. As presented and dealt with by
most Christian educators, these are matters of indoctrination. There
is an attempt to secure certain ends without providing a body of experiences and opportunities for critical creative thinking which might
make the ends meaningful and dynamic. In spite of the fact that
every penny carries the slogan "In God we trust" there is no agreement, among theologians or laymen, as to the concept of God. It is a
vague term around which endless controversies center. Likewise,
there is wide difference in interpretation of the life and teaching of
Jesus, and the theological arguments about salvation and atonement
are hopelessly involved. The phrase "Christian interpretation of the
universe" recalls the bitter fights between science and religion with
the attempts to make some preconceived idea of God determine beliefs about the observable facts of the universe. Similarly, there is confusion about the other goals, with conflicting opinions as to the
nature and importance of the Bible and the church and with radically
different meanings for, and methods for attaining, a Christian social
order and a Christlike character. All these objectives suggest im-

portant ends for religious education, but they imply indoctrination as the method for realizing them and ignore the learning process by which meanings grow, ideas are refined, and motives are aroused. They tend to make religion a conformity to patterns of verbal expression and vague loyalties rather than intelligent appreciations, growing insights, and satisfying commitments.

It is sometimes assumed that the first question of children will be theological, but this is not true. If they are in an atmosphere in which the term God is repeatedly used, they will want to know what God means. But when a child asks who made the sun or what makes the flowers grow, the needed answer is not in vague theological terms. And to take advantage of such questions to introduce the term God is not religious education. Children need to understand the processes of life, to respect the wonderful, complex character of these processes and to feel the possibilities of becoming acquainted with them and of working with them. As they grow and as knowledge widens and deepens, they need to feel more and more at home in the universe, to sense their place and value in the total scheme of ongoing life, and to get satisfaction from asking questions and thinking with others on the interesting, though often perplexing, problems of life.[4] In spite of the fact that the Hebrew-Christian varieties of religion have on the average been higher than most others, it should not seem necessary to set all religious ideas and values in terms of these traditions. As in general education, not only do we need acquaintance with prescientific religious concepts, the classical biblical ideas, and historical forms, but we also require investigation of why people believed as they did in olden days, what additional knowledge we have today of the world processes, what history has to tell us of the meanings and worth-while goals of living, and what the best judgments are in our own era. Religion has always been functional when it has been vital, but it has not always had the same body of knowledge, social facts, and problems to deal with; and so it has been different in each situation where it has formulated theologies and practices for group use. Hence, it must remain a quest without authoritative and fixed concepts, institutions, or mores.

The common assumptions that religion deals with the "supernatural" and that truth is "revealed" must be subject to free critical inquiry. Neither term can be defined so that all who claim such belief agree on what is meant. What some call "supernatural" is simply an inference from incomplete knowledge of that which others call "natural." Both the supernaturalist and the naturalist live in the same world and have many common experiences, and both seek as large fulfilment as possible of their lives. The naturalist may value the orderly creative forces of life and the spirit of love, justice, and dependability without either personifying them as God or assuming a divine being as portraying these characteristics. To some, religion is worship of an assumed God; to others it is an attempt to get an appreciation of the cosmic resources and to understand the inherent laws and possibilities of life. And as for revelation, naturalists believe that anything which may be "revealed" must be interpreted and understood in terms of the rest of life or it has no significance for them. Both concepts, "supernatural" and "revelation," lie in the field of emotional experiences, which have not been critically studied. To the naturalist and functionalist, religion cannot put a premium on the vague and not-yet-analyzed experiences of life without being discredited by persons accustomed to critical thinking. If experience teaches us that we live in a universe where there is unity, the basic truths of religion must be discoverable in the observable facts of life.

As people explore the possibilities of personal-social living, the gap between the growing ideal and the existing state of human affairs steadily widens. For some the religious solution is a miraculous intervention by an assumed deity and the perfect fulfilment in another world after death. For others the proof of spiritual realities is in their power to be realized in the present life-process. The achievement of social and economic justice, the establishment of peace and good will among men, the correction of crime tendencies, the refinement of sex, the mutual respect of persons for each other in the varied relationships of life, the enjoyment of the beauties and abundant privileges of a good world by everyone, and other ideals are being increasingly realized while the means for their further attainment are being sought. Religion is appreciation of the resources and laws of growth and commitment to a co-operative way of living, without any feeling of wanting a deity to reduce the responsibilities of intelligence.

To sum up the steps in the development of this quality of religion which we have called the quest, we present the following needed processes of religious education:

1. Answer the questions of inquiring children, youth, and adults by directing attention to the learning opportunities in formal and informal education, to the opportunities for direct observation of the processes of an orderly world, and to the possibilities of experimenting and evaluating with the best known ways of living, in seeking the basic meanings and worth of life.
2. Encourage critical and creative thinking, helping growing persons to find the secrets of progressively satisfying procedures in the everyday activities of co-operative living.
3. Help growing persons to get the perspective of history, to feel the slow growth of comprehensive spiritual values and the skills of religious living, and to be able to identify and to use the manifold privileges for personal-social enrichment.
4. Provide guidance by trained persons in the evaluation of ancient concepts and the development of religious ideas and practices so that the distinction may be appreciated between temporal forms and underlying realities.
5. Show how the functional interpretation of religion is in harmony with the quest of the ages and represents the pervasive and continuous spirit of living religion in all centuries.
6. Let the problems and fields of study in religious education be graded to the widening experience and maturing development of people, without confusing young children with theological abstractions and without prejudicing appreciations by indoctrinating methods of teaching.
7. Give frequent occasions for recognizing the progress in religious understanding and in the skills of living spiritually so that the quest may prove rewarding and revealing.

INTEGRATION OF EXPERIENCE INTO A WORKING
PHILOSOPHY OF LIFE

The essential complement to quest is integration, for experience comes piecemeal and is not fully understood until it is put together, permitting the pattern of life to appear. Religion seeks to view life as a whole, to appreciate its total meaning and worth, so that the perplexing problems of particular and changing events may be comprehended. To the degree that universal and enduring qualities can be discovered, what is called the divine plan is revealed, and one can feel a sense of stability and security. A functional analysis and re-synthesis of experiences on a continually widening scale must reveal whatever evidence there is of abiding principles and laws and must test whatever deductions are made from theological conceptions. The fact needs to be kept constantly in mind that whatever supernatural-ists call God is based on their experiences of the universal order, but these ideas need to be subjected to critical analysis as knowledge of the universe grows. Whatever generalizations are made by a nat-uralist must also be checked by growing experience and by inter-action with other free minds. The religionist seeks a working philos-ophy with a theory of the nature of the universe and of man, a set of values related to full and free living for all persons, and a de-veloping code of morals for personal and group conduct. In the modern world of critical thought, with theories being continually revised in all realms of knowledge, the religionist needs methods for integrating and revising meanings and values based upon this chang-ing body of ideas.[5]

The first experiences of life are organic, without reflective thought, being unified by the central nervous system. That which happens in one part of the body is felt throughout the organism and conditions the operations of every other part. Each part has a special function to perform, but there is a flexibility in the operations of the parts and of the whole, permitting adaptation to varied needs and environmental demands. Throughout life, organic tendencies and habit patterns probably control attitudes and acts more of the time than rational principles and consciously controlled purposes. Consequently, religious education must be just as much concerned with the conditions which affect these organic tendencies as with those which determine one's fluent verbalisms. The confession of Paul, "The good which I would do, I do not; but the evil which I would not, that I practice," may be a fairly general human experience, but it does not justify inconsistencies or wrongdoings. Paul felt that he had learned how to master himself to some degree, but the theological explanation which he gave would not be considered as a good psychological diagnosis today. He might have thought that with the mind he could "serve the law of God" and with the flesh "the law of sin," but no one who has studied human behavior carefully believes that mind and body can be so separated. Neither does a realist believe that the conflicting tendencies in one's life can be resolved by some mystical acceptance of Christ, for the divine law written in the very nature of human development is that repetition follows satisfaction. As long as one finds more satisfaction in treating a person of another race with contempt than in showing him respect, the organic tendency is to show contempt, whatever one may tactfully say. Race relations will be on a basis of mutual helpfulness when people actually find satisfaction in working together. True spiritual development is an integration of one's feelings, rational attitudes, and habits of behavior. The functional approach recognizes the fact of organic integration and seeks to correlate closely beliefs and practices, correcting any tendencies to disintegration. It seeks, therefore, to further those situations in which constructive social attitudes and acts find satisfaction and to modify conditions which prevent the growth of spiritual appreciations and consistent behavior.

This does not in the least discount the value of reflective thought, for man transcends the lower animals in his capacity to be critical and objective concerning his attitudes and acts. It is the task of good education to teach people from the earliest years to be self-critical, to conquer tendencies to be two-faced or hypocritical, and to find satisfaction in integrity and sincerity. By reflective thought a man can see himself as others see him, can identify traits in himself which need improving or correcting, and can hold himself toward significant goals. One does not simply will to be integrated, and one does not achieve integration by mere meditation or prayer. It grows by continually joining reflection to action, and doing so in close proximity to the situations in which action has meaning and emotional quality.

Thus, children have to talk things over with parents, teachers, or older persons who can help them to see things in perspective and to work out satisfying principles of action. A group of youngsters who were quarreling over marbles were asked to tell a supervisor what was wrong. By skilful questioning the children were helped to see that they needed rules, and they worked out a few simple regulations for playing which gave them larger freedom and enjoyment. Good athletic coaches teach young people to consider the best principles of team play. Strict rules are inflexible, but, when players get the principles underlying co-operative skills, they can adjust to changing situations with greater effectiveness. In a civics class a teacher may give descriptions of laws and regulations observed in civilized society or may help students to work out the basic principles necessary for a well-ordered society and stir within them discontent at unsatisfactory social conditions. Labor leaders may stampede their members into strikes and violent actions to attain justifiable changes in wages or working conditions, or they can educate them to appreciate the complexity of economic conditions and make them willing to move slowly without imperiling the welfare of others. In every phase of the common life we have the problem of using reflective thought to build working principles, respecting human values at every turn and seeking integration in the forward march of mankind. We do not get very far by having Sunday discussions of abstract righteousness and Monday battles of practical adjustments in which Sunday principles never emerge because they have never had any vital, vivid connection.[6]

Mental ability to reflect, to analyze, and to resynthesize experience grows slowly, but with the steady accumulation of ideas and the necessity for organization of basic principles evaluative skills must be developed. Out of the host of things which happen in a day or week, only a few things are remembered, and it is always a question of what is important; for small incidental things seem to make more difference, frequently, than time-consuming operations. Hence, the need for reviewing experiences, for careful evaluation of them, for building norms and goals, instead of drifting along and letting things happen. Religion looked at functionally is this process of review and evaluation, reorganization and redirection of a highly complicated growing process. It must not be allowed to degenerate into a merely verbal conformity to general truths which others have formulated. Worship should dramatize the critical experiences of living people, cause reflection, stimulate group-mindedness and readiness to deal with current problems. It is harmful when it becomes a substitute for clear thinking and sustained effort or when its meditations are divorced from the duties and privileges of ongoing life. There are too many things in our cultural systems which tend to retrograde unless special attention is continually directed toward concrete problems.

It is the field of religion to re-evaluate all values which control the welfare of the people, to uncover unappreciated but available values, and to correct false allurements. This means that religious services must do more than emotionalize general goodness, for there is little dynamic in such formalities and no guidance for dealing with specific situations. For instance, it is easy to idealize honesty, but in our complex economy one does not know how to maintain strict honesty and participate in a social order where business and government continually compromise with fair and just practices. Or, again, one may be kind in meeting a particular need but at the same time be unjust to someone else who has a greater need and right. Some think that the

Christian way is so simple that one can say to a child, "Follow Christ, and you will not do wrong." But when Jesus cleansed the temple of its money-changers, did he violate an important principle when he used violence instead of an appeal to reason? Is his precedent dangerous? Religion must encourage the best training that can be given by homes, schools, and other agencies of our democracy in keen analysis of problems of moral conduct and of programs involving human values. The integrity of one whose mind is kept alert by such influences is much more difficult to maintain than of one whose moral attitudes are vague sentimentalities.

We live in a world where compromises are inevitable and where people make different adjustments without ever getting satisfactory basic principles. This situation was especially acute during the war, but there are many confusing issues in everyday relationships. The conscientious objector refused to fight but seldom had any constructive plan for meeting the military aggressor and took a course which, if others had followed it, might have led to the destruction of democracy and to the multiplication of other evils. The conscientious loyal citizen who hated war as much as any C.O. compromised with his ideals to meet a situation in the most constructive fashion which seemed practical in the emergency. The Golden Rule and the Great Commandment, "Love thy neighbor as thyself," are both compromised in practice, for it is impossible to share one's possessions with all people in need. Most Americans could do with much less if they actually cared about starving millions. Even a small sacrifice on a national scale would render relief to a host of people, but how many churches are advocating any sacrifice? It is easier to worship a sacrifice than to practice a sacrifice, and the rising generation has probably less of the spirit of sacrifice than the older generation who lived on a more disciplined schedule. We need to help young people feel that religion is more than platitudes and more than weak compromises. It must express and direct growing social adjustments so that progress can be made and integration be achieved on higher levels.

General educators are approaching the problem of integration from several different angles. One of the most hopeful moves is the collaboration of persons working in different areas of traditional studies of human behavior. Thus we have psychologists, sociologists, anthropologists, and biologists working together and making their findings meaningful for general education. The general purpose is that with a better comprehension of the growth process and the factors affecting it we may organize our education and gradually modify our cultural patterns so that integration of personality may take place on continually higher levels. Organized religion needs to keep abreast of these moves, conserving and furthering everything of this nature at all age levels.[7] A virile brand of spirituality does not attempt to escape from the difficulties of living in a world in which distances are shrinking and interrelated problems are increasing. This is a welcome offset to some theological defeatists, whose only hope is in a cataclysmic change or a radical modification of the present order. In addition to seeking better integration within school curriculums, educators are endeavoring to relate school learnings to general life-activities at all age levels. In the adult period we find many schemes for informal education to enrich the general culture of a community and to relate domestic, vocational, recreational, civic, and other interests. Co-ordinating councils and a few other experimental agencies have shown how readily many people respond when opportunities are provided for integrating community activities.

One of the unfortunate moves in general education has been the attempt, usually under pressure from outside interests, to introduce religion into the program of the public school as a formal addendum in dismissed or released time. Several plans have been tried but with much divided opinion as to value even among the advocates. The reasons for trying to introduce religious teaching into the public school program are varied but include such arguments as the following:[8]

1. Delinquency records in many of our communities are alarm-

ingly high, and it is hoped that religious teaching may help to correct evil tendencies and to develop better ways of living.

2. Churches are enrolling less than half of the children and young people of America, and those who are enrolled attend irregularly. There is a desire to reach the unreached and to provide one hour a week more of religious instruction, and it is hoped that public school influence will help.

3. Many want children to know the Bible because it is God's Word or because they do not want their children to be biblically illiterate. They hope trained teachers may be able to give their children good Bible teaching.

4. Many hope that religion may be better integrated into general education by this kind of contact with the public school.

All of these desires—to correct delinquency, to give more children opportunity for religious education, to know the Bible, and to bring religion into operative relationship to educational objectives—are worthy ends; but there is a failure to understand the essentials of religion and to appreciate how it functions constructively in lifting standards of life.

The following criticisms of the weekday systems are indicative of their weaknesses and shortcomings:

1. They are sectarian, dividing a community and destroying the united democratic spirit of the public school. Ordinarily, children in public schools do not have to wear labels of Jew, Catholic, Baptist, Christian Scientist, Lutheran, or whatever their parents have chosen to wear or have inherited.

2. These systems assume by their very organization that whatever the Protestant, Jewish, Catholic, or other sect teaches about religion is equally good, as long as each is tolerant of the other.

3. Majorities repress minorities, ignore their rights, and deny religious and democratic principles in order to get their way.

4. There is no critical evaluation of religious teachings, no examination of basic assumptions; and the whole process tends to be a

blurred sectarian interpretation of religion given by an uneducational method of indoctrination.

5. Weekday systems of religious education fail to give due recognition to the functional characteristics of religion which might be meaningful to children and youth in the regular program of the public school, giving primary attention to theological, biblical, and ecclesiastical phases of religion.

6. They assume that physical proximity to general education will integrate religious ideas and values, disregarding the psychological laws of learning.

7. They give a false interpretation of religion as something which can be added to general education by a one-hour-a-week program, failing to lift out the spiritual elements which pervade all good teaching.

Instead of the artificial plan of weekday religious education on released time, churches need to revise their regular teaching periods, making them more effective and interpreting religion as a pervasive quality of all life. Further, the public school should be encouraged to identify and to make significant the ten types of experience which we have outlined or some such functional analysis of religion. The need for helping young people to respect and to use religious principles is illustrated by a news item published recently. In a city of many churches, where weekday religious education on released time has been in operation for years, a group of five hundred high-school boys and girls went on a strike as a protest against Negroes' being allowed to attend the same school as whites. Undoubtedly, these young people knew the religious ideals about race relations, but their knowledge did not function in this critical practical situation. Social sensitivity and the rest of our basic religious experiences must be developed in living adjustments which start in the home, are taken up in the kindergarten, and continue throughout life. No formal schemes of religious education will make them dynamic and pervasive. We are steadily moving toward the day when such problems as this race issue will become primary problems for general education and when other agencies, including the church, will be asked to co-operate. As we have shown in our discussion of these ten types of religious experience, the public school has many opportunities to make them meaningful and to develop these spiritual qualities, without entering upon any controversial religious arguments. Either the churches must awaken and take the lead in sensitizing educators to their responsibilities or the general educator will put the church on the defense.

Throughout this book we have tried to make religious objectives specific, to indicate how they can be illustrated in every relationship of personal-social living, and to show that if such a functional naturalistic interpretation of religion becomes pervasive, we may have a true integration of life around expanding creative interests. We have lifted out under each category definite principles for a working philosophy which may be adapted to the comprehension and needs of persons of all ages and backgrounds. In doing this we have demonstrated the methods by which people may growingly come to appreciate these values and outlooks on life and to weave their own experiences into a meaningful whole. There is no hope for integration and unity by conformity to a creed or custom, but there is a growing proof that these functional elements of religion leaven society. The lines of progress are not inevitable for any individual or group, and even nations may pass away and be forgotten except for a few relics; but the process of growth is inherent in the nature of the universe, and those who learn to obey its laws may expect to benefit thereby. The picturesque final judgment in which the goats and sheep shall at last be divided must give place to a judgment that continually separates those who find the enduring qualities of life from those who miss them. Millions are born every day. Millions die every day. A working philosophy of life must be built out of the living experience of those millions. The question, "What makes life worth living?" must be answered by reference to history, not by theological assumptions.

Chapter Seven

History and Celebrations

RELIGION functions impersonally as well as personally, through social mediums as well as through direct social interaction. The kind of religion that individuals and groups exhibit is conditioned in large part by the traditions and customs preserved in language, symbols, records, worship practices, festivals, and other group celebrations. People become accustomed to these from childhood, build meanings and associations into them, and accept these conventional signs as identifying marks of religion. Use of theological terms, performance of formal rites and ceremonies, and reverent loyalty to orthodox formulas and patterns are counted as fundamental for a good Jew, Christian, Moslem, or member of any faith. One may have moral traits and measure up very well in the other eight categories which we have outlined, but in many people, if one fails to express one's self in fairly regular fashion, there are suspicions of heresy and disloyalty. Likewise, in patriotic attitudes flag-waving and fluent verbal gestures are more often watched than sacrificial acts and intelligent, co-operative relationships. When an appraisal of religion in an individual is desired, the first reaction is to prepare a questionnaire to discover how much he knows of the Bible, how regularly he attends church, what theological statements he accepts, and what he knows about denominational tenets. There is seldom any attempt to appraise religious attitudes, conduct, or intelligent appreciation of meanings and forms. Secondary characteristics are important, but one must be careful what inferences are drawn from them.

In these last two types of experience we remind ourselves of the need to keep individual reactions in a racial setting. This means more than a sectarian, or particular doctrinal, point of view and is more than most people are ready to accept. What we are, what we think, and what we emotionally prefer are dependent upon the influences which are carried along in the social stream in which we live. People are likely to forget that even the word God is a social heritage, and the particular kinds of ideas associated with the word are the result of social usage, even as the words for food, and thoughts related to the verbal symbols, vary with different geographical and social areas. One thinks and feels about religion very differently according as one is brought up in an orthodox or reformed Jewish home and synagogue, in a liberal or conservative Christian community, or in any other religious, or irreligious, environment. One's religious outlook, meanings, values, and goals depend upon the total cultural setting and upon the particular religious ideas and forms with which one is familiar. The conditioning social factors may be either assets or liabilities, but in most situations they are a somewhat confusing medley. One desires to profit by the cumulative wisdom of mankind, but it is extremely difficult to separate temporary forms and archaisms from abiding truths and to evaluate critically the varied expressions of closely related ideas and attitudes. The main trouble seems to be that few people are trained in the art of critical, constructive thought, and few know how to differentiate facts from interpretations or reality from emotional impressions of it.

In an article about the German nation, Lord Vansittart said, "Once a cliché is in their heads, not even experience, let alone argument, will get it out again."[1] This is just about the situation in religion, and what we are discussing in this chapter is of critical importance in considering possibilities of improving the sad state of religious anarchy in the world. Presentation of this functional point of view to a minister of a leading church in a major denomination, where his laymen were much interested in the possibilities of transforming their church-school programs, brought as the first reaction, "Brother, that sounds well, but where is the revelation of God in Jesus Christ?" This preacher had once been a liberal, but he had swung back into a conservative orthodoxy and was rotating around two or three theological formulas. He had ceased to think critically and, like an infallible pope, asked all to bend before his gilded images. Discussion of meanings and functional significance of terms were secondary to use of the theological formula. One has to be very careful lest a particular image, or an emotionally wedded phrase, block out all sense of reality. It is possible to hold a nickel so close to the eye that one can shut out the sun and the rest of the universe. Language and symbols should be tools, not tethering-posts, while forms and ceremonies should be artistic mediums and not determiners of concepts. All records handed down in written form, institution, or custom must be critically examined and related to ongoing experience. Any statement of belief, customary procedure, or organized agency must be regarded as instrumental, subject to changing comprehension and needs. Truth can never be confined to a dogma, or cliché, without losing its fundamental quality of growth and vitality.

In the last two categories we are especially desirous of emphasizing the creative character of religion, first, as it arises in the individual in his interactions with others and with the records of the past or present and, second, as it emerges in group experiences in times of celebration. The processes involved here will continually affect the other eight kinds of experience which we have defined. The functional approach keeps all phases interrelated and prevents traditions and variant forms from smothering the living spirit of religion.

APPRECIATION OF HISTORICAL CONTINUITY

One's mind (and soul) is the resultant of cumulative experience. Ideas, values, ways of adjusting to living situations, growing ability to analyze and resynthesize, failure and success in meeting problems, all contribute to the sensitization and working power of the individual to think and act with what is called intelligence. Mind is the organizing and directional center of personality, and its functioning is organic and dynamic. It does not operate as a wax cylinder or disk, repeating impressions; but it weaves together the many strands of experience, uses consequent meanings, restlessly seeks further knowledge, and constantly deals with changing problems. It can objectify experience, compare and contrast factors and processes, choose between alternative procedures and elements, and deal creatively with any object or phase of reality. But mind is not limited to representation of things as they are, for it has imaginative powers and can combine into fanciful pictures any set of factors. It is difficult for most people to keep the two types of ideas, fact and fancy, separated, and many do not want to do so.

A child enjoys letting his imagination work at will and in the period when he is dependent on others can indulge this free play of fancy. But as life takes on responsibilities and reality must be faced skilfully and courageously, he finds it necessary to discover the resources in the real world and to make imagination a servant rather than a master. This maturation of mind and discipline of critical creative thought are essential to the fullest operation of religion. One of the biggest handicaps to progress is the lamentable fact that few people have developed their capacity to think, reacting most of the time on a primitive level instead of on an educated, refined, intellectual, and appreciative basis of thought.

Instead of seeking to deal with the universe in terms of its inexhaustible and richly stimulating nature, people are likely to picture a limited and repressive system under control of an arbitrary deity. Instead of investigating and experimenting to find the most rewarding ways of living, many assume that ecclesiastical rules and regulations are divine laws. The oft-repeated objectives "to foster a consciousness of God" and "to get right with God" are vague shibboleths; for the concepts and images of God are numberless, and any indoctrinating method of religious education which assumes a particular view shuts out thereby a true adjustment to experienced reality. To further an uncritical belief in deity is no more religious than to cause children to believe in fairies, demons, or brownies. Many investigations of common ideas of God reveal a fantastic lot of imagery, and unless the symbol is given specific reference, one cannot expect anything else. If "God" is a term used to designate integrative, creative, and personality-sustaining cosmic power, the important thing is to indicate the evidence on which the concept is built. If other terms, such as "Father," "Love," "King," "Lord of Hosts," "Holy Spirit," "Shepherd," or any of the endless list of ascriptions are used, the factual basis on which a universal cause or controlling power is assumed should be given. A symbol and a hypothesis should not be substituted for a knowledge of reality.

The nature of the world processes as discovered in daily experience, through scientific study or in historical surveys, is more important for man's adjustment than any imaginative concept of deity. A scientist or historian who appreciates and respects the resources of his world and seeks to realize fulness of life for himself and others may be as religious as the theologian who talks about God. The common man who profits from his daily experience and tries to be true to the best that he knows may be religious in spite of whatever theological indoctrination he may receive. One may use the term "God" irreligiously, fancifully, or intelligently and reverently.

So with the use of the Bible, one may have simple, naïve beliefs regarding its supernatural character, or critical-historical understandings of its nature, values, and relative significance in the story of religion. There is no inevitable religious experience in Bible study; for, as is well known, the Bible has been used to justify all kinds of evil, and many people have only a smattering of cultural knowledge without any appreciation of its inspiring teachings. There are various reasons for the widespread attachment to the Bible, but undoubtedly one of the main reasons is the traditional belief in a supernatural God, who was supposed to have given this book as a revelation of his will and purpose for man. The only justifiable use for the Bible from a religious standpoint is one in which its historical and developmental character is fully appreciated and understood and in which its insights and patterns of behavior are critically evaluated. One is not necessarily religious when he employs the gangster tactics of Samson, the fanatical attitudes of Jeremiah, the dogmatic spirit of Paul, or the violence of Jesus in expediting reforms. The Bible is an interesting book, portraying the developing religious ideas of a small group of people in ancient times. There are innumerable other books in the literature of the ages, and more to be written, which may serve the purpose of helping young and old to think and to live religiously. To treat the Bible as a unique and isolated revelation of truth is to deny the essential quality of growth in the cosmic process and to ignore the experiences of the vast majority of people as inconsequential. The Bible must take its place in the vast array of religious literature and, without presumption as to uniqueness, prove its worth by the insights which it gives to intelligent and receptive minds.

Religious education may well include critical-historical studies of the Bible for young people and adults, and this can be given in more stimulating and enlightening fashion by well-illustrated lectures than is usually done in the piecemeal discussion of incidents and isolated passages. People should realize that it is no more religious to take a text from the Bible and read into it some moral or spiritual teaching than to take a sentence from a daily newspaper and make it the instrument of a homily. Most people who want more Bible either desire cultural knowledge or are interested in the sermon attached to a biblical passage. They do not know how to use the Bible as a source book for religious history and as a resource book in developing religious ideas and moral principles. Biblical scholars have done much to make the Bible a living book and intelligible in the light of its ancient social setting, but most preachers and teachers ignore their findings.[2]

Religious educators should feel free to draw illustrations from biography, history, poetry, science, or any other source which can throw light upon the nature of the universe and of human problems. In the Appendix we shall show how a church-school curriculum may be enriched by the use of many different kinds of materials, when the end points are defined in living, functional terms. The Bible is not neglected but is studied in a comprehensive and functional manner. A naturalistic view of religion permits one to examine all types of literature, to find stimulation and guidance from many kinds of experience. Many living characters and social situations present more inspiring religious lessons for children, youth, and adults than most of the Bible can be expected to give; and the transfer to everyday living is much more direct. Instead of thinking of religion as something supernatural, archaic, foreign, and talked about chiefly in church or by theologically minded people, it is discovered as a vital quality in every adjustment of life.

If the world is to become one brotherhood, with understanding and respect of each nationality, race, and class for each other, the spirit of religion must be far more pervasive and uniformly expressed than it is at present. A functional approach offers better opportunities than trying to get agreement in theology, church doctrines, and institutional practices. We need co-operative studies in all the areas we have described, with language, symbols, and literature that can further common thought and action. Two world wars have driven men and women to the constructive task of organizing a just and peaceful social order, but this spiritual ideal needs the backing of religious people who have faith in human worth and its growing capacities. In its present state, organized religion is divisive, controversial, and tangential to the main course of the social order. While freedom is essential to the full growth of religion, this does not mean that a luxuriant growth of weeds is as fruitful and efficacious for human needs as crops produced under scientific study and care. If we are to avoid anarchy in religion, we must educate people to see that theories and practices in religion need as thorough examination and refine-

ment as all other phases of human experience. Fanatical propaga-
tion of irrational beliefs and programs makes a mockery of religion
and hinders appreciation of the truths and values which ought to be
more fully understood and respected. The basic functional characteristics of religion which we are describing in this whole book are
qualities which have universal appeal and are capable of unlimited
expansion as human knowledge and experience grow. Thus, faith in
the worth of every individual and desire for every person to realize
his full capacities are basic challenging ideals for every nation and for
all mankind. Two world wars have tested this spiritual concept,
modified many attitudes, and presented a colossal task to religious
leaders. Social sensitivity is the only atmosphere in which this worth
can be realized, for we must have people who can think of themselves and others at the same time and find satisfaction in the experience. For some it is unbelievable that those of different race, nationality, class, and enemy status can be treated on the basis of the Golden
Rule and respected on the basis of worth and potentiality. Yet religion
which lacks these two elements is superficial.

Other factors are important and can be developed more readily once
these two primary qualities begin to grow. To attain this growth, we
need to take advantage of the many situations in which face-to-face
contacts are made, co-operatively working to solve common problems
and to further mutual interests. From a functional angle the religionist
must be interested in the many occasions of war and peace, economic
and social relationships, political and personal adjustments, when people of different types have to meet, be courteous to one another, work
out reciprocal agreements, and put into writing mutual understandings. Many aversions, prejudices, and misunderstandings are over-
come as mind challenges mind, generosity evokes like response, and a
sense of significant co-operative attainments is achieved. It takes more
than a Christmas legend and a song to effect "good will among men,"
and yet we need songs which can be sung around the world, songs
which will stir vision, hope, and action. In the days ahead it is impor-

tant that conferences of educators, labor leaders, athletic and recreational directors, economists, artists, scientists, social engineers, and many others be held to stimulate international-mindedness and to afford many happy occasions for creative and co-operative thought and planning. Such meetings may not necessarily displace ecumenical councils, but at least they may give needed outlets for the ecumenical spirit. If we could by-pass intrenched theologies and ecclesiastical structures, we might make much faster gains, organizing new religious ideologies to meet world needs. There is nothing peculiarly religious about the Hebrew-Christian language or ideology, and religion might make greater progress if this were once acknowledged.

The free critical discussion of beliefs and practices gives people opportunity to discover that the Hebrew-Christian tradition is not one clear-cut faith in one God with differences only in secondary matters of church customs but that the very concept of God is a hypothesis which never has been uniformly expressed. Religion is not adherence to a vaguity but a faith which persists and grows as interchange of experience, analysis of past records, and critical creative thought make increasingly definite the latent potentialities for personal-social living. The fact that mankind throughout the ages, in all countries, has developed interest in these problems and has sought for the way of fulness of life is a greater stimulus to faith and endeavor than the story of one little section of humanity who believed that they were chosen for a special revelation. A sound religious faith can rest better upon universal factual data than upon isolated interpretations of isolated segments of experience. A growing religious faith needs the growing integration of the best experiences and thought of people of widely differing backgrounds rather than the rationalization of the latest hunch of a theologian or self-designated prophet.

Religion in a modern world is a weird collection of strange ideas and customs, but underneath lies the search for cosmic meaning and universal principles on which the co-operative life of interdependent people may reach its maximum. Hence in this functional view of religion we are concerned with every creative discussion which seeks to put political, economic, educational, journalistic, or other human relationship on a universal scale of values. We have an inductive approach to determination of religious principles rather than a deductive, based on theological presuppositions. From this standpoint what takes place in a manufacturers' association, a labor congress, an educational convention, a political rally, an economists' conference, a military council, or any large meeting concerned with human interests is as vital to the shaping and functioning of the religious spirit as any gathering of preachers, theologians, or sectarian advocates. To do his work effectively the religious educator must watch these varied situations and seek to conserve, integrate, and direct the most promising lines of spiritual growth. We need community, national, and international religious movements which shall transcend the ordinary circumscribed interests of sectarian organizations.

Lastly, in this section on appreciation of historical continuity, we desire to emphasize the implications of changing from theological indoctrination to this creative interaction of outreaching, intelligent minds. The unregenerate ecclesiastical systems which assume that people can be made religious by talking to them and causing them to conform to stereotyped expressions must give place to democratic institutions which promote free critical thought, stimulate people to reach ever higher levels in all phases of daily living, and help to keep perspective and integrated purposes in all personal-social relations. This means that religious education ceases to be a pouring-in process, giving young and old theological, biblical, and moral knowledge, that it does not depend upon some mystical work of divine grace for personal-social transformation, and that the basic laws of growth are respected. From the earliest years growing persons must have satisfying experiences in working out reciprocal adjustments, formulating co-operative principles of living, choosing personal objectives, judging outcomes, and taking responsibility for the improvement of the status quo. The process of religious education must be visualized as taking place in homes, schools, leisure-time agencies, political organizations, business and professional relations, and other social activities. The effective church will stand at the center, a radioactive community, inspiring faith, keeping sensitivities keen, and continually helping people to be conscious of the cosmic setting and universal meanings of life.

PARTICIPATION IN GROUP CELEBRATIONS

The word "celebration" sometimes suggests a primitive kind of emotional release when intelligent, disciplined attitudes and conduct are relaxed and unchecked desires are loosed. People get drunk, do all kinds of foolish things, lose their individualities in a crowd, and give vent to pent-up feelings. The thin veneer of civilization is cast off, and animal appetites assert themselves. Intelligence is given a vacation as the restrictions and refinements of culture are shaken loose. After a big celebration it is tragic to read the reports of crime, accidents, and foolish waste. A good time for many means that the thresholds of intelligence are lowered, critical judgments are at a minimum, and reckless feelings are indulged. History reveals that even religion has frequently degenerated into wanton debauchery, sex perversion, and irrational forms of behavior in times of ecstatic demonstration and intense emotional excitement. Thus the true quality of religious celebrations has as wide a range of values as that of other human behaviors.

At best, religious celebrations are refined expressions of deep appreciations in which intelligence is joined with emotional response. They help to prevent life from becoming drab, meaningless, and directionless. It is so easy to get into ruts, to do things mechanically, and to miss those things which give life zest and purpose. Yet life holds great possibilities for all, for we live in a world of inexhaustible resources. Many never discover the finer meanings and thrilling adventures of great enterprises in which they may have a significant part. They need a dramatization of opportunities, vivid contrasts of the high and low life, stirring reasons for appreciations of what they have and of what is available to them. They need visions of what co-operative living may be in the varied relations of life and stimulation to make themselves assets in the social order. Celebrations which are carefully planned and democratically enacted may do much to arouse people from sluggish indifference or from mediocre living and to keep them sensitive and responsive to worth-while endeavors. They may put things into perspective, give them the needed color and attractive lure, and develop in people a feeling of working happily with others for desirable ends.[3]

Religion has its major and minor forms of celebration, its regular and special times, places, and ceremonies. In the Christian faith there are many customs that are shared by the different sects, but each one has special days and ways of celebrating. The Jews have their list of holy days, with appropriate ceremonies for each; and all the other religions of the world have feasts and festivals and worship customs. The concepts, practices, and attitudes involved in these various forms reflect social backgrounds and culture and are of distinct interest as a revelation of how religion springs from the primary needs of man and is not handed down from heaven. In all these celebrations man acknowledges dependence upon a power or powers greater than himself and shows desire to maintain fruitful relations with this environing source of his welfare. In much worship the deity is exalted, but in the very ceremony and emotional experience man also seems to find exaltation and incentive to creative effort. The expectations from worship and other celebrations vary greatly from naïve magical types of attitude to the most philosophical. The magical attitude prevails in far more people than is usually recognized, for the emphasis upon certain authoritative forms, formulas, and administering personnel suggests the same kind of irrational expectation that is sought in a mimetic dance or by the use of amulets and incantations.

From a functional standpoint and in keeping with the philosophy which is being outlined in this book we would indicate the possibilities of worship for developing phases of religious experience supplementing those already described. In so doing we assume that worship may be formal and informal, private and collective, occasional and regular, graded and general, with endless adaptations to particular needs. The basic elements which we feel should grow in worship, enlarging its meaning and effective use and increasing its intellectual insight and maturing personal-social qualities, include the following: (1) growing appreciation of the magnitude, resourcefulness, order, and meaning of the cosmic processes of life in which we live, move, and have our being; (2) growing understanding of the nature and latent possibilities in personal-social development, with increasing interest and desire for maximum attainments; (3) sense of the value of meditation, reflection, perspective, clarification of main objectives in individual and social living, and organization of purposes and plans, under conditions which experience proves are enriching and stimulating; (4) developing of group attitudes and insights to support and to further individual strivings for the realization of expanding ideals; (5) growing appreciation of the refined, aesthetic enrichment of life by music, art, literature and other carefully prepared forms for articulation of ideas, ideals, and emotional responses; (6) utilizing of conventional and traditional words and forms to express common faith and purpose, with continual revision through critical social thought and experimentation; and (7) a balanced use of scientific data, poetical imagery, critical thought, and receptive appreciation to combine the verifiable facts of experience with the mystical colorings and overtones which characterize all nonsuperficial reactions.

For the naturalist, God is not an imaginary supernatural being, but the word is the name for the most important phases of one's cosmic environment on which personal-social life is dependent. God is not denied, and the naturalist is neither agnostic nor atheistical but functional, adjusting himself to the creative, orderly processes of life which he experiences in daily living. He finds satisfaction in systematic exploration instead of bowing to some vague image. Worship is not an induced mystical hypnosis but a refined appreciation of supreme value and a commitment of life to their realization. The naturalist can express his feelings and attitudes in prose or poetry, but he does not forget nature's laws, or the actualities of life, when he becomes poetical. One may speak of, or to, God as one addresses his country, or an abstract ideal, in poetical symbolism, but one must always recognize the danger of reverting to anthropomorphic concepts and of conveying such impressions to others. The child and primitive people personify experiences readily and do not distinguish between reality and image. The naturalist may be just as reverent, grateful, idealistic, and outreaching as any supernaturalist; but his conception of reality and the processes of growth may be quite different.

In beginning with the little child the religious educator will be concerned to have him experience the wonders, beauties, resources, and possibilities of life in his real world. He will teach the child to reflect, to analyze situations, to compare and contrast factors and experiences, to see things in relationship, and to profit by what others have learned. He will endeavor to help the child feel the value of these periods of worship in gaining meanings, a sense of inexhaustible resources, and an increasing ability to solve problems and live worthily. As children pass into adolescence, and on into adulthood, the religious educator will seek to stimulate them to explore life more fully and to commit themselves to significant tasks. In doing this, worship will be a means to give vision and purpose, orientation, perspective, and motivation. Functional sensitivity will prevent worship from becoming meaningless gestures, mystical dreaming, or merely aesthetic enjoyment. To this end there is need of systematic education in the meaning, techniques, social forms, and materials used in worship, with revision of prayers, hymns, ritual, procedures, and settings consistent with the kind of naturalistic philosophy we have discussed.

Many things have been done to make worship more meaningful and attractive, but only a few people have been willing to make radical changes in words and forms and to prepare people for their effective use. Most hymns multiply strange imageries, "cherubim and seraphim," "joy of heaven," "angel guards," "chariots of wrath," "the Lord in his holy temple," "Father, Heavenly King," "Lift us to the joy divine," "thine alabaster cities gleam," "Lead us, O Father," "Till we cast our crowns before thee," and like terms. Prayers repeat petitions of "Help us," "Teach us," "Strengthen us," "Take away the love of sinning," "Deliver us from evil," "Be gracious unto all mankind," "Feed the hungry, and care for the homeless," and other similar requests, without any suggestion as to how these needs can be met. There seems to be little relation to ordinary laws of development and dependable order in the attitudes of worship. We need expressions of faith in a world that science has explored and in which history has kept the record of human progress. Prayers should be meditations, statements of appreciation and faith, and commitments to worthy living. When confession of shortcomings or failures is made, it should be with regret but also with confidence in the possibility of doing better and with purpose to profit by experience. Our services of worship should have more thrilling recitals of heroic living than they now have, more stirring pictures of worthy achievements, and more challenging portrayals of things which should and can be done. People need to be disturbed in their complacency, roused from lethargy, and impelled toward unselfish service for the common good. Instead of multiplying references to an assumed deity, worshipers should recall the facts and experiences which have given life its largest meaning as well as the problems which block satisfying progress, and in the light of the total picture should express faith, desire, and purpose. Let us use pictures to aid in the visualization of tasks and resources, striking charts and graphs to aid in the appreciation of achievements and to map out lines of advance, and dramatic presentations to make vivid the contrasts between unworthy and noble living.

Outside the varied forms of worship let us consider the opportunities for significant religious experiences in other types of celebrations.

We have the general religious holidays observed commercially, recreationally, and religiously, such as Christmas, Thanksgiving, and Easter; special festivals and holy days in the different sects and synagogues, such as Lent, Passover, Purim, Epiphany, and Michaelmas; observances such as the Lord's Supper, baptism, installations, ordinations, dedications, and anniversaries; national commemorations such as Independence Day, Memorial Day, Columbus Day, Lincoln's Birthday, and Labor Day; various other celebrations such as weddings, birthdays, community anniversaries, Valentine's Day, Children's Day, Mother's Day, Hallowe'en, and New Year's Day. All these have possibilities for religious education, recalling important achievements, noting crises in history, exalting human values, sensitizing people to significant relationships, stimulating high endeavors, and generally causing reflection upon meanings and opportunities frequently missed in the common day's routine. Sometimes these occasions degenerate into times of tiring emotional excitation without enduring values, or they are allowed to pass without any refreshing or constructive use. Too many people are chained to their daily tasks and get into humdrum ways of living, without taking time to enjoy the beautiful things in their world, to explore some of nature's interesting secrets, to share friendships with people of varied talents and qualities, and to do things with others that will make life richer and better in the whole social order.

Some families plan for good times together on birthdays, anniversaries, holidays, and sometimes on Sundays. Individuals are given special recognition, family ties are strengthened and happy memories are built up; initiative and talents are called into action, mutual understandings are developed, and philosophies are shaped in discussions and activities richer and larger than the ordinary day's interactions. Schools make a great deal of patriotic events, civic and national celebrations, graduations, special assemblies; and, among younger children, schools do even more than churches to give meaning and remembrance to Christmas, Thanksgiving, and Easter. There are very definite spiritual interpretations given to historical events, critical turns in individual and group life, social responsibilities, and worthy attainments of both pupils and outstanding contemporaries.

Churches have always done something out of the ordinary to mark special days, and the response has been indicative of popular interest in religion. People do not find much value in the ordinary services, but they enjoy a celebration, good music, something dramatic, and sharing in a crowd reaction.

Communities tend to celebrate a few times a year, and the spirit of togetherness and general good will transcends separate interests and divisive prejudices. Rural districts have annual fairs, husking bees, bazaars, musical festivals, 4-H Club rallies, and other traditional events. Small towns and residential urban sections have a wide variety of celebrations, exhibits, garden shows, Thanksgiving services, Christmas trees and singing, picnics, patriotic parades and programs, anniversaries of local institutions, Labor Day demonstrations, band concerts, and athletic meets. A few holidays are national, and from time to time special celebrations are federally initiated; for such events many agencies tend to co-operate while radio and press endeavor to develop common interests and action.

In all these occasions there are latent possibilities for spiritual insight, enlargement and refinement of values, and closer identification of individuals with each other and with the common welfare. The religious leader may frequently capitalize on these types of experience in his church program, but he may more often find opportunities to influence attitudes and interests by participation in community affairs and by direct influence in preparation for such events and in review of what was accomplished. The radio, press, pulpit, forum, public school assembly, clubs, church school and other organizations, all offer opportunities for discussing principles, stimulating creative interaction of minds on important problems, and promoting a spirit of friendliness and hopefulness in which constructive changes can be made to advantage. In recent years intercultural festivals have been developed in schools, churches, labor unions, clubs, and all-community groups. These have been especially good in releasing tensions, giving outlet for talents, lifting differences to the level of community assets, and providing friendly occasions for general acquaintance and good will.

Some of these celebrations give opportunities for recalling past achievements and enjoying customs that have been forgotten. Some provide stimulating situations for creative talent, for a new appreciation of the fast disappearing present, and for discovering latent resources in ordinary people. But the main need in planning a project, developing it, and bringing it to a successful conclusion is to give as many people as possible chances to share in it creatively and cooperatively. There are many books and articles suggesting ideas and giving patterns, and one does not have to travel far to find a great variety of talent, but the art of making a good time a spiritually invigorating experience requires careful cultivation and an artistic spirit. Religious leaders need imagination and a capacity to help others see and enjoy things which they have never fully appreciated but which will continue to awaken happy reflections long after the festive occasion.

Chapter Eight

A New Day for Religious Education

THE atomic bomb has shattered traditions and expectations. People will have to think in new terms, and the possibilities of changes in the next hundred years are far greater than in any period in history. Will religion become a side-show museum of antiquities, or will it be a faith and an integrating spirit ever rising to higher levels of vision and purpose? The problems of religious education in this critical turn in world events are tremendous and intimately related to the whole future of mankind. Can we through orderly educational processes enable a sufficiently large body of people in all parts of the world to think creatively in spiritual terms related to the needs of mankind in order that longings for a better world order may be realized without delay and bloody revolutions? Under our present systems of organized religion there is very little unifying influence and just a pathetic demonstration of socially transforming power. The latent spiritual forces are operating in a diffuse manner without clear united objectives and effective agencies. Too much time, thought, and energy are being spent in keeping obsolete machinery from falling to pieces and in discussing and refurbishing outgrown ideas. Religious education is needed, not to propagate traditions and to keep people divided on ancient sectarian issues, but to help people organize new ideas and attitudes and to bring into effect new policies and programs.[1]

Let us first of all recall what religious education means. It is a systematic, planned procedure for making religion meaningful and operative in individual and collective living. It involves determination of objectives, recognition of the laws of human growth, development of effective methods and materials, training of personnel for leadership, and planning and revising programs in the light of carefully evaluated outcomes. Objectives depend upon basic philosophy, concepts of religion, constituency needs, and available means for attaining specific ends. They are both immediate and far-reaching, specific and comprehensive, and must include all the agencies that are interrelated in their activities. Psychological understanding of processes must be developed, for it is no more foolish for a farmer to scatter his wheat over a paved street and to expect a good harvest than for religious leaders to ignore the laws of spiritual growth and to expect significant changes in individuals or society. There is a mystery in the development of plants, but no intelligent farmer depends upon prayer and mystic experiences to produce good crops. He studies soil, climate, seed, processes of development, machinery, prices, labor, and other factors that may affect the outcomes of his farming. The more he knows, the more intelligently and effectively he can do his work. Likewise, the religious educator needs to know how habits and attitudes are formed and changed, how ideas and ideals take shape and become influential, how emotions arise and are controlled, what socioeconomic factors are operating at a given time in a given situation, and other important elements in the contemporary social process. These are revelations of the divine methods and laws and need to be as reverently studied as any biblical records of ancient ideas and mores.

The day should be past in which theological seminaries give main attention to reproduction of ancient ways of thinking about religion and to abstract speculations about prescientific concepts and in which they isolate studies of Bible, theology, and church history from studies in the nature and needs of growing people and changing society. Many ministers and theologians who took courses in college psychology seem to be immune to psychological principles and critical habits of thought. They become fluent in words, masters of logic and illustrations, and fail to probe beneath their presuppositions or to come in contact with a living process. Religious education should be at the heart of all seminary training, the point of view testing the worth of all learnings and the measure of vital interest in people and their welfare. It should check the tendency to use religious words as if they had magical power and should give insight and skills for working co-operatively with living people in a real world. Good intentions without enlightened knowledge and critical judgments may not produce heavenly qualities.

In the foregoing chapters we have outlined a functional and naturalistic view of religion and have given many illustrations as to how religious growth is taking place. We have identified religion in action, showing how it operates in the commonplaces of human relationships, and we have discussed the possibilities of a greatly expanded program of religious education. In this chapter we gather together and develop some of these inferences to make explicit what is meant by "A New Day for Religious Education." The picture is not of utopia but is a realistic portrayal of what is going on and what can be practically developed under intelligent direction. It will seem radical and fantastic only to those to whom religion is blind faith and to whom religious education is a plan for indoctrinating the rising generation with what one has been taught. To many it will be what they have always felt was the underlying and vital spirit of religion.

Before elaborating the principles and policies which we believe will be increasingly manifest in progressive fields of religious education, we shall summarize what we regard as critical developments: (1) The primary need is a growing faith in the spiritual resources of our natural world, with an increasing sense of the comprehensive unity of experience underlying a religious interpretation of life. Religion is not supernatural conjectures but life lived at a maximum in a knowable universe that stimulates personal-social growth. (2) A close correlate to this naturalistic faith is recognition of the pervasive and identifiable nature of religion. We believe that the functional aspects of religion are the major concern of most people and that they are the final norms for religion and religious education. Theologies at best are speculations built out of experimental data and should be kept secondary to the evidence which gives them birth. (3) An increasing knowledge of psychology and of critical methods of thought is essential to the refinement and growth of religious ideas and attitudes and to freedom from traditional supernatural concepts. People must learn why there have been so many different beliefs and what is the basis for a growing dependable faith. (4) Historical perspective is important for gaining a right appreciation of the meaning and values of religion in the progress of mankind and for having confidence in the world-wide search for truth and the realization of the latent possibilities of a dynamic universe for all kinds of people. (5) Recognition must be given to the many different agencies in which people may discover and express religion, and the special function of the church must be defined as an integrating and inspiring fellowship in local, national, and international life. (6) In a comprehensive program of religious education much depends upon the possibility of helping parents, teachers, and leaders in all areas of our common life to become sensitive to spiritual qualities and skilful in promoting their growth. (7) Effective educational methods must be kept in tune with a growing basic philosophy by utilizing the best techniques and materials available. (8) Enrichment of experience will be furthered by wise and artistic use of historical and current literature depicting the problems and achievements of spiritual advance. The Bible will be one important source among many in a well-graded curriculum for the varied needs of young and old. (9) A gradual transcendence of sectarian and divisive interests will be achieved in the multiplication of co-operative enterprises and in the clarification of functional goals. (10) The liberal, progressive spirit of religious education will become more attractive as it proves its practical comprehensive power and draws into co-operative relationship leaders and workers from all areas and interests of our complex world.

The move from supernaturalism to naturalism is slow; for no one ignores the fact that man has been produced, and is sustained, by forces greater than himself. The real issue is how to designate that power, or powers, and what attitude to take toward it. The primitive reaction is to personify, but a critical mind gets little satisfaction in putting a marvelously complex process into a vague conceptual image. Through long, careful study man has come to a fair understanding of his universe and its developmental processes, and it seems a useless oversimplification to call the determining and controlling cause of it all a personal God and to imply anthropomorphic characteristics in every reference to him. It is confusing and, the naturalist believes, irreligious to define "spiritual" as a series of operations outside the natural and observable processes of life. When the supernaturalist assumes a deity, either immanent or transcendent, or both, who creates man and keeps in touch with him by miraculous means different from the regular experiences of natural life, the naturalist questions the reality and value of such imaginary constructs. He looks around and finds an endless multiplication of gods in America as well as in every other land. The educated American smiles at the ignorance of uneducated people who can worship gods of wood and stone but fails to realize that the shelves of every library are cluttered with as many gods as are in India or Africa. In every American seminary we have devotees who worship at different shrines, some at Professor X's latest creation and some faithful to older favorites.

The naturalist recognizes the personality-producing forces and the dependable orderly processes of the world in which he lives, moves, and has his being. He deals with experiential facts rather than with hypothetical inferences and seeks to be as exact as he can in reference to the processes of creativity, mutuality, integration, and progression which he finds in his world of experience. Prayer is neither an appeal to a power outside the natural for manifestation of divine will nor an attempt "to lift one's self by one's bootstraps" through wishful thinking. It is a meditation, a consideration of problems and needs, a recall of experienced resources and a reorganization of one's mind and attitudes for more effective working in a world of plural possibilities. The naturalist may, or may not, use the word God in his prayers, but when he does it is with a definite reference to processes of reality which he desires to keep in mind as he orients himself for optimum adjustment and fullest realization of appreciable values. He guards against dualistic concepts of sacred and secular, divine revelation and natural revelation, inspired and uninspired, saved and unsaved, supernatural and natural, and puts his faith in a creative, evolutionary process in which differences are relative and progress is gradual. He does not live in fear of the arbitrary acts of a temperamental deity but in humility and unpretentious dignity because he feels his personality is respected, his intelligence is significant, and his possible contribution to the evolving world order is thrilling.

For the naturalist, religion is dynamic, unifying, evaluational, without any feeling of having to conform to a fixed divine order in blind submissive faith. There is freedom in a world of plural possibilities; there is responsibility under the law of the harvest; there is hope and invigoration in being a partner in an inexhaustible creative process. Religious education that is to help growing persons live spiritually in their real world of daily experience must speak in terms which honor the natural processes and which integrate the learnings from all of life. It must be specific and concrete, normative and directional, motivating and energizing, and always developmental and adapted to particular needs and situations.

With the functional approach one seeks to catch the spirit of the seekers of truth of all ages and to carry it forward into the rapidly moving and perplexing present. We ask what has functioned most satisfactorily in the growth of human values and relationships and what has been most meaningful and dynamic to human progress. We find that our answer is not merely in the conventional and organized expressions of religion but is more truly in the attitudes, values, and behavior patterns of everyday living. We have outlined them in our ten basic experiences, and we recall their significance for the new day in religious education:

Sense of worth.—In spite of tragedies, sufferings, and discouragements of every kind we find that man has kept an invincible sense of worth, with a growing appreciation of the possibilities for human development and a desire to realize the fulness of life. Whoever, or whatever, stimulates this spirit is an ally and asset in the furtherance of spiritual growth. We find helpful forces in homes, schools, juvenile courts, hospitals, employment agencies, counseling clinics, churches, and many other situations; and we find need for clearer vision and better methods of guidance.

Social sensitivity.—One is almost astounded at the growth of this spirit, for it is operating on a world scale of relationships. In the Old Testament we find little expectation of the Golden Rule operating beyond tribal lines; and even in the New Testament, Peter had to have a "miracle" to widen his sympathies. But today we realize that two world wars are the result of failure to practice social sensitivity on a large enough scale; and we see businessmen, politicians, and the common man trying to take the role of people who have hitherto been nothing more than impersonal objects in their world. We find many movements to better intercultural relations, to meet racial conflicts, to improve economic conditions, to give the underprivileged different status and opportunities. Mutual respect, love, and brotherliness are spreading, and the spiritual agents are multiplying; but much remains to be done, and in many specific situations one sees need for careful experimental advance.

Appreciation of the universe.—The traditional measure of religiosity by testing theological orthodoxy is giving place to evaluation of one's intelligent appreciation of the orderliness, responsiveness, and developmental character of the world and its interrelated processes. Reverence for the product of human imagination and verbal skills is being displaced by deep respect for the beauties, wonders, and creative forces of one's environing world. Instead of religious education imposing theistic beliefs upon immature minds by indoctrinating methods, the modern approach is to help growing persons integrate the varied experiences of their world into a working faith which will expand with deepening insights and widening knowledge.

Discrimination in values.—In this area we see the chance likes and dislikes, attitudes and values of young and old subjected to analysis, evaluation, and refining educational treatment. Norms are developed relative to personal-social values, and re-evaluation proves the worth of sacrificing lesser for greater gains. The degree to which this quality of religion has become a working part of one's philosophy and action is another test of the maturation of spirituality. A little child may grasp its principle in a limited sphere while an educated adult may still find difficulty in differentiating some values and in being willing to pay the price for highest achievements. Most follow the fashion, or line of least resistance, refusing to cultivate higher capacities.

Responsibility and accountability.—The difference between the traditional expectation of unquestioning obedience to authority, whether home, school, church, state, or God, and the modern attitude of intelligent discriminatory co-operation is hard for some to appreciate. When authority is relative and unquestioning obedience is not a virtue, responsibility and accountability take on new meanings. When religion exalts freedom and democracy as conditions for the best growth of spiritual qualities, these two factors become significant. Self-discipline and consideration for others with whom one must co-operatively work is a *sine qua non* for life above the regimented and compulsory level. Religious education is interested in every effort to make people ready for the use of freedom and democratic interdependence.

Co-operative fellowship.—Because most of one's life is lived in groups it is important to develop a sense of identification with others of one's primary groups and to have the spirit of a co-operative enterprise in all group relations. This should be just as true of one's home, neighborhood, school, club, business, political organization, state, nation, or other social relation as of one's church; and in each case the spirit of fellowship should be governed by spiritual ends. It is hopeful that today many see the need for working on an international basis in the United Nations Charter and other agreements and that the startling effect of the atomic bomb has accentuated the imperative necessity for closer ties. Hundreds of agencies are trying to further the spirit of co-operative fellowship—counseling clinics, labor arbitration boards, antidiscrimination organizations, luncheon clubs, conferences, settlements, churches, interfaith councils, and religious educators must keep in touch with such movements in order that theory may become practice and that the ideals of the kingdom of God be actualized in transformed social life.

Quest for truth and realization of values.—There is no more functional aspect of religion than the spirit of the quest; for it is man's ceaseless searching, experimenting, testing, and evaluating which have made him dissatisfied with traditions and the attainments of his ancestors and have led him to deeper insights and higher ideals. In its further development religious education will not ignore the past, but it will not depreciate the present to exalt the past. It will expect to stimulate search for better theories and practices. It will honor the scientist, the pioneer, the radical, or anyone who pushes forward the boundaries of knowledge or raises the standards of living. It will seek to awaken the interest of growing persons in front-line social problems and to strengthen faith in greater possibilities for more people. It will try to reduce the defensive attitude and the fearful attacks of conservatives, helping them to find the fun and satisfaction in adventurous living.

Integration of experiences into a working philosophy.—As one tries to put the facts of life together, to get underlying meanings and patterns, there are plenty of problems, but the solution is not to say, "It is the will of God." Modern religion seeks to find principles that operate in the whole of experience and the relation of particular events and experiences to the ongoing totality, in so far as it can be comprehended. One seeks goals, consuming interests, and enduring satisfactions in the midst of disturbing and perplexing inconsistencies of good and evil, suffering and joy, justice and injustice, wealth and poverty, life and death. Religious education cannot satisfy the mental and emotional needs of growing persons by presenting them with authoritative absolutes in general abstractions but must start with young children, helping them to draw conclusions from experiences, to test and revise these in the light of their own further experiences and those of others, and to feel that there is order and reason in all things. The modern teacher does not give belief in God as the basis for this confidence but shows that the evidence of history, science, art, religion, and daily living supports a trust in the cosmic process.

Appreciation of historical continuity.—The importance of objectifying experience and of subjecting impressions, feelings, and emotional beliefs to critical judgment is stressed in modern religious education. The fact that there are so many different beliefs and practices and that religion is so divisive should cause people to welcome careful examination of assumptions, vague statements unsupported by evidence, conflicting beliefs, traditions, and authoritative claims. The free exchange of ideas is growing as sermons, services, and exhortations crowd radio programs and are published in many forms. But there is not enough open-minded critical study of these varied teachings, for most seem to want reasons for going on thinking and acting as they have become accustomed rather than seeing things from a new point of view and finding more comprehensive principles and more satisfactory unifying theories and practices. Instead of trying to read teachings for every person and every need into some Bible passage, modern religious education aims to develop a true appreciation for the Bible and also a broader acquaintance with the spiritual treasures in other historical and contemporary literature. The new day in religious education should bring music, art, symbols, exact language, ritual, inspirational and study materials, with methods of improving and adapting them to particular needs, all expressive of the functional and naturalistic meanings of modern religion.

Participation in group celebrations.—Though many have exalted worship as the chief function of the church, the norms seem to be concerned with choir, preacher, and social atmosphere. In the new day, religious education will need to cultivate deeper meanings and desire for more specific outcomes. Both private and public worship, for young and old, may be richer and more stimulating experiences than most stereotyped practices tend to be. A basic religious philosophy must underlie any effective use of worship; and, yet, well-planned worship services will help to develop the philosophy. Both regular and special celebrations help to keep the primary facts and ends of personal-social experience central and attractive. They give life needed perspective, keep it from retrogressing to mediocre and low levels, add dignity and worth to both individual and group activities, and further confidence in a progressive world order.

Another critical development for a new day in religious education must be in understanding the principles of social psychology. People need to know that ideas, attitudes, values, habits, and emotional experiences are all conditioned by their social environment. One speaks English with a New England accent, loyally supports a Republican administration, abhors lies or lies cheerfully and well, holds prejudices of a certain kind, goes golfing summer Sunday mornings and to church on Easter Sunday, because of social influences more than rational purposes. People need to know how ideas and attitudes grow and change, how sects have arisen and why they continue, why different theological concepts appeal to different persons, why the Bible has been called God's Word, and what the uniqueness of Christianity is. There are too many general attitudes for and against religion which have no rational justification and too many ideas that are vague and without real substructure. There is little use in calling conferences for interfaith collaboration if the several members of the conference have no ability or desire to understand their own presuppositions and ways of thinking, let alone those of others. Many meetings seem to be little more than friendly gestures of blind people or gracious tolerances of self-satisfied isolationists. In most interfaith meetings there is no expectation of gaining light on truth and of changing one's ideas, though there is a willingness to exchange tricks for propagating what one has. Once a person has been indoctrinated with a particular brand of supernaturalism he tends to remain a Catholic, Baptist, Christian Scientist, Mormon, Buddhist, or Jehovah's Witness, as long as he lives; and there is very little difference between the several basic assumptions. If one is willing to face the "divine" facts of psychological growth of ideas and attitudes, the truth of this will be readily recognized.

The new day in religious education must teach people to think critically, constructively, and fearlessly in all matters of life—social, political, economic, moral, and religious. If people are going to use the word God, they should understand its varied meanings—a beautiful legend, a working hypothesis, a symbol of specific cosmic forces, a personification of an ideal, or whatever else is implied in its use. If the Bible is used, it should be studied critically and historically to appreciate its origin, its conflicting moral and religious teachings, its developmental character, and its possible values for a questioning mind. If loyalty to a church is to be developed, it should be on a free democratic basis, with each member free to ask questions and to offer suggestions for the improvement of teachings and practices, programs and enterprises. If religion is to become a functional, integrating experience helping persons to weave together a meaningful life-pattern, to gain growing appreciation of life's possibilities for themselves and for others, and to move co-operatively toward their ideals, it will do so as intelligence is used at a maximum and as man acts with discretion and vision instead of under social pressure and with blind feelings. Psychology is a study of how people become human and grow to fulness of humanity, what the laws and conditions affecting this growth are, and how such knowledge may be used in an educational process.

There is a great deal more history to religion than what is contained in the Bible; and if religion is to become a normative, directive, and cohesive world force, religious leaders must know more and use more. Hebrew-Christian ideas and practices were determined in large part by their social environment, and they have been greatly modified through the centuries by contemporary world views and social conditions. The majority of the people of the world have never been Jews or Christians, and yet their experiences and religious outlook on life are important. In the days ahead when all civilizations are merging, and interdependent relationships are multiplying, it will be especially desirable to respect the religious heritage of others and not to try to impose some particular brand of Christianity on them. The religion needed in China, for instance, is surely something different from that which might satisfy the liberal wing of the Northern Baptist Convention of the U.S.A. or the fundamentalistic section of the Southern Methodist Episcopal Church of the U.S.A. The functional approach and the naturalistic interpretation of religion give us abundant opportunities to transcend the traditional speculations of the past, while still recognizing their values for past generations, and to make a definite spiritual contribution in the reconstruction of a new world order.

It is easy to criticize the people of the East for worshiping their ancestors and their ancestors' gods, but most of the people of the West look backward for their religious ideas and inspiration. East and West alike need to have confidence in a present which is ever moving out of the past and yielding more wonderful meanings and greater possibilities for personal-social living. If it were not so, it would be useless to turn back, for what is enduring is significant in the present. If we take these ten areas of basic experience, we find that every period of history, and every culture today, has something to enrich and to inspire nobler living; for these phases of religion are perennial and pervasive. Today, after the devastation of war, millions are seeking a new recognition of worth, a kindlier social sensitivity, a new faith in the reconstructive processes of their world, norms for enduring values, freedom and a chance to prove their responsibility, significant and secure fellowship, evidence that their quest is not in vain, principles that transcend the tragedies that threaten to overwhelm them, confirmation from the experience of others that the struggle is worth while, and opportunities for the mountain-peak experiences which give life perspective and hope.

Religious education has unlimited resources in the stories of mankind's achievements and in the concrete instances of those who have triumphed over injustices, sufferings, and tragedies of all kinds. In any land and among any people, young or old, there are plenty of illustrations of what religion means; and there is no need or desirability to try to make the Bible, and especially Jesus, teach everything. Living pictures from the pages of history are far more stirring than abstract doctrines and outgrown theories. We need well-illustrated books, biographies, period studies, stories of the growth of ideas, interpretations of ancient and modern customs, records of social struggles and heroic acts, dramatic contrasts of worthy and unworthy living, vivid epics, and unforgettable poetry. Every land can contribute valuable human experience; and home, church, and school can make use of the products.

In the expanded program of religious education, homes and family living may be transformed. Young people may be taught how to prepare themselves for the important role of homemaking and personality-building. If our ten basic experiences are analyzed in terms of what good home life may do for a man, his wife, children, and friends, it will be found that rich and varied possibilities are available for every type of situation. There are gigantic problems in population control, economic distribution, domestic relations, housing, yearly wages, and cultural development, which are all related to what family life may contribute to spiritual elevation of mankind. These are not merely academic questions for social scientists or practical adjustments for labor, management, and politicians. They are critical issues for religious educators who believe in the processes of growth and do not let ideas of supernatural intervention block intelligent, creative work. This means that if homes are to become effective religious agencies, religious educators must work co-operatively with social scientists, government leaders, labor representatives, educators, industrial executives, social workers, and others who have power and opportunities to help shape better home conditions. The spiritualization of society is slow, as the centuries prove, and formal church services are only one small part in the total process.

What we have said about the family is largely true of other social institutions, for each is dependent upon the others; and what people do in one, affects what they can do in others. Religion is a pervasive quality—the gradual appreciation of values, the constant leavening process which changes all behavior. At one time, and in one place, religious education might do well to give special attention to ways of helping adolescents to face the privileges and responsibilities of marriage and homemaking; and at another time and place it might take an interest in a psychological clinic for parents, a campaign for a decent living yearly wage, or a housing project for a crowded section of a city. When this comprehensive view of religion is taken, educators will think in terms of conferences, institutes, cooperative projects, direct and indirect influences, and the conditioning factors peculiar to different situations and age levels. Instead of setting ministers and missionaries, social workers and reformers, in a class by themselves, the new day should see every vocation dignified and sanctified by its responsibility for human welfare. There is no profession, trade, or service which cannot make significant contributions to the enrichment and ennoblement of life. We need to identify spiritual opportunities and responsibilities, to lift out sample acts which either advance or hinder spiritual growth, and to make people sensitive to their obligations as democratic spiritual beings. The writer has done this many times with camp directors, Y secretaries, public educators, parents, and student groups; and it can be done with individuals or groups of any kind. The functional analysis of religion in action deepens the meaning of religion, distributes responsibility for its operation, and gives larger reason for expectation of specific results.

The problem of leadership training is broadened from this point of view, and methods and plans must accordingly be revised. The present systems of professional training for ministers, religious educators, missionaries, Y secretaries, and social workers are too limited in their horizons, too narrow and unrealistic in their programs and purposes. There must be basic changes in social psychology, social philosophy, and religious philosophy, as well as in practical methods. One essential is development of co-operative attitudes, ability to work with others, respect for what other people can and must do in intelligent and sympathetic unity, and specific planning for joint actions. Another requirement for these religious specialists is enough acquaintance with other fields to invite co-operative undertakings and to express desired end points in language meaningful to all. The functional interpretation of religion will be found to be much more flexible than the theological and more vital to the combined efforts of people of different position, training, and outlook. The foundations of leadership training should be in home responsibilities, school assignments, play activities, and ordinary citizenship duties. In a democracy everyone should find opportunities for initiative and furtherance of the common good without waiting to be ordered and driven by others. Leadership is a relative term, for one may be a leader in one activity or cause, and a follower or humble partner in another.

Because a democracy does provide freedom for initiative, we have the constant problem of persons assuming leadership who are inadequately prepared for the role which they take and of others following them in uncritical, sheeplike fashion. Many are stimulated to participate in a religious or humanitarian movement that is ill-conceived and perversive of wholesome interests. We come again to the need for training in critical thinking, analysis of presuppositions, and careful weighing of issues and methods. The public school, college, and university, at all levels, should develop skill in scientific and creative thinking; and they should do more for specific leadership training. Leaders need knowledge, vision, skill, and emotional drive, with an unfailing interest in and respect for those whom they would inspire and lead. Emotional enthusiasm and human sympathy are usually products of social contagion, but the spirit is finest when it is joined to a keenly critical and alert mind. Education is not adequate or complete until all pupils have purpose and sense of ability to be of specific worth in their community, and in varied social relations. Homes, schools, churches, press, radio, and other agencies must all work on this problem of developing social expectancy and of stigmatizing nondemocratic responsibility. Many educators are defining their objectives and planning their programs to further these ends, and many churches are moving forward in their conceptions and plans for better leadership; but there is an unequal balance between intellectual factors and the other qualities which we have identified. We need both plus specific training for special needs and functions.[2]

In the field of methods we stress first that end points determine the means that should be used. When critical creative response is desired rather than conformity, indoctrination cannot be accepted as a method. When religion is regarded as a quality of a growth process, there will be no fear of losing a faith or of failing to achieve a loyalty when freedom of thought is encouraged and expectation of growth in appreciation and insight is taken for granted. Democratic procedures will be desired in all education and in all social relations, and churches will not have reason to operate on any other basis. The question as to whether there should always be a core curriculum, with electives to meet individual needs, may persist in religious circles as well as in general education; but the necessity of making all curricular offerings, at every age level, living and interrelated is imperative. Whatever is to be learned should be meaningful and supported by rational data. Religious teachers must not ask statements to be taken on faith or authority alone, and traditions must be carefully examined whenever they are offered for acceptance and use. To do otherwise would be as foolish as for a science teacher to be dogmatic or to offer outgrown theories as modern truths.

In presenting facts, demonstrating relationships, and motivating conduct, the religious teacher must welcome modern techniques such as audiovisual aids, dramas, radio programs, forums, charts, pictographs, socialized reports, sampling polls, use of pictures and illustrated books, and booklets. There is much to be done in assembling suitable materials to enrich a functional program. We need examples at every age level, and in varied situations, of persons proving their worth, demonstrating social sensitivity, profiting from study and wise use of the laws and resources of their natural world, sacrificing lesser for greater gains, and in all these ten areas of finding satisfying and exemplary experiences. For worship, assemblies, and festive occasions we need songs, pictures, rituals, stories, suggestive plays, discussion outlines, and resource materials which may be used to make functional aspects of religion vivid and attractive. The imagination and creative talents of religious leaders must be developed in order to go far beyond the limited traditional range of materials in church-school and young peoples society.

In particular, we need illustrative methods of using current events, and of dealing with significant writings in science, philosophy, psychology, sociology, history, and general literature. From the standpoint of religious education we are concerned with advances in knowledge which reveal the nature of our universe and the processes which affect our whole welfare. The atomic bomb has revolutionized the attitudes of people toward war and international relationships, and further discoveries in atomic energy may change socioeconomic life more than anything in ten thousand years. Religion must keep pace with the meaning of these changes for human adjustments. To go on saying the same prayers, repeating the same ritual, and rehearsing Hebrew-Christian history will not suffice for the spiritual needs of the modern age. Recently, conferences on the interrelations of science, philosophy, and religion have helped to stimulate interest in the necessary inter-weaving of learning from different fields of reseach; but we are still a long way from religion's being considered a functional element of all life and a responsibility of all persons for incorporation of its principles and attitudes into every phase of human relations.

When religious educators cease making religion coextensive with Bible knowledge and theological fluency and actually come to grips with the problems which ongoing life presents, they may expect to get co-operation and intelligent interest on the part of thinking men and women in every sphere of life. Our curriculums must include at all age levels materials which draw from the best literature, past and present, to illustrate aspects of spiritual living and to stimulate and guide thinking and emotional response. In the Appendix we give a report of one experiment which has been made to widen the base of source material and to organize a curriculum on a functional basis. Religious education committees, conferences, and organizations should include representatives of different fields of human interest and learning; and projects of research, study, curricular planning, social action, and educational procedure should reflect the broad and deeply penetrating spirit of religion.

In doing this, we shall have reason for transcending the present sectarian and traditional patterns of religious organization and expression. We shall have to do more than has been done in the past, though some may think that we have achieved a good bit in our interdenominational, undenominational, and interfaith projects. The Federal Council of Churches of Christ in America, the International Council of Religious Education, the National Conference of Christians and Jews, the World Council of Churches, and many other organizations do show tolerance and a measure of good will and co-operative action; but they all assume that religion can be compartmentalized and that people are justified in maintaining traditional ideas and practices as the basis of organization and operation. The past will be honored best when it ceases to be an anchor and becomes a springboard. If there has been no growth in concepts, meanings, and basic programs in two thousand or more years, religion is too dead to be of concern to anyone, and its remnants should be carefully preserved in museums and archives. If it has grown, its modern forms should be richer and more vital for modern living. Mergers of denominations are good, and multiplication of common interests and co-operative enterprises are better than isolated activities.

But we need more and something quite different. The center of religion should be in efforts to achieve fullest possibilities of personal-social living, not in trying to keep loyalty to a vague body of pre-scientific ideas. The test of the vitality of religion should be in its pervasive, integrating, and transforming spirit. The maintenance of organizations and the bond of fellowship should receive incentive and purpose from both expanding insights and objectives and also from the critical needs of changing world conditions. There is too much waste energy, exhaustion of emotions, and loss of religious enthusiasm in an attempt to maintain harmony in denominations and to keep people polite to each other when they are wearing sectarian labels.

It is just as foolish to try appeasement methods to keep religious peace between fundamentalists and modernists, Protestants and Catholics, Hindus and Moslems, as it was to shut our eyes to political differences before the second World War. Most sectarian organizations could be scrapped to advantage in local, national, and international religious reorganizations. We need religious centers in every local community, in which the community may express its spiritual ideals, its unity for common welfare, and its faith in a progressive order. We need an institution which is free from the state and free from hierarchic controls, which can invite free interaction of minds, with critical, constructive attitudes and programs. We need larger organizations joining persons of varied vocational interests, those of different race and national backgrounds and those of varied talents, who desire to work together on matters of spiritual concern. Instead of measuring one's religiosity by his membership in and loyalty to a static organization, let it be in the participating interest one shows in humanitarian causes, social problems, and development of interesting programs of religious education for young and old. Worship programs and group celebrations may be radically revised and serve to focus interest and thought on the central issues of religion and of life. Sectarian groups have served useful purposes, though none too well; but the old forms are inadequate, and merely minor changes will not suffice. There will never be uniformity in religious beliefs or interests, but freedom for fullest development of the finest qualities of religion is not being realized by the perpetuation of a host of archaisms.

Liberals and progressives in religion do not need to be on the defensive. They should let conservatives build whatever Maginot lines they will and glorify whatever traditions they will. We live in a dynamic world, in which atomic forces shatter old notions of security, in which the masses of the people are awakening and asserting new desires, and in which critical creative thought is imperative. We live in a world not of one Book but of many significant books, not of one religious culture but of plural concepts and practices, not of one God but of many gods. Liberals and progressives will do well to work together on common problems, to find bases for growing bonds of fellowship, to encourage freedom but to guard against anarchy. The Allied Nations won a great war by pooling resources and breaking precedents; the atomic bomb was produced by a combination of international scientists; the hope of the future is in a spiritual unity directed to specific tasks of gigantic size.

Appendix

An Experimental Curriculum

Throughout this book we have offered constructive suggestions for changes whenever adverse criticisms have been made. It is not enough to censure theories and practices as outgrown and inadequate, for he who finds fault with existing conditions should point the way to something which he regards as better. Further, the new should be developed in living situations where human adjustments temper fine-spun theories. We have too many productions in the field of both general and religious education which are only slight variations of conventional types, without contributing anything significant to the growth of educational practices.

In the matter of curriculums this is especially true, as any survey of materials will show. With the launching of this functional analytic approach to religious education we have felt an obligation to indicate what this might mean when used with children and youth in the programs of a church school. At a later time it may be possible to illustrate what can be done in home and public school situations. The experiment described below assumes that the church may be an important agency in helping to shape ideas, attitudes, and values, if its educational program is articulated in functional terms closely related to everyday life. It therefore departs radically from the traditional forms where biblical and theological ideas are central and organizes its lessons about the ten basic experiences of our functional analysis of religion.

The experiment in curriculum-building began after conferences and preliminary studies with two ministers of a local church. They and their church-school staff collaborated for a period of nearly three years. As the project advanced, a number of other churches joined forces; and the different situations in varying denominations, size of schools, types of workers, and general backgrounds gave excellent opportunities to test out materials and methods. Owing to difficulties in getting adequate help in writing and in supervision of teaching situations, the outcomes are definitely limited. Yet the study reveals a number of significant things for curriculum-building, which seem to justify the brief report given herewith. It makes clear that there is an inexhaustible mine of resources for developing lesson materials at every age level. It shows how religion can be made meaningful and vital for current living without having to relate every lesson to a biblical incident. It uses the short-unit technique to stimulate intensive studies on the wide range of topics which need to be considered in the complex situations of modern life. It seeks to integrate the learnings of home, school, church, and other community relationships.

The curriculum is organized on what is called a unified functional basis in a three-year cycle, with lesson units on a departmentally graded plan. Eight of the ten basic experiences have been used as centers of interest in developing units. Elements from the other two, "Integration of Experience into a Working Philosophy" and "Participation in Group Celebrations," are being woven into other units for the time being, though each of these is just as suggestive as the others for lesson topics. The units consist of six lessons on a departmental topic related to a general theme for the whole school. For instance, during a period of six weeks a school gives attention to those phases of religion which we have called "Sense of Worth"; and in the first year the general theme is entitled "Spiritual Possibilities in Growing

Lives." The kindergarten has six lessons under the general topic "Children Grow and Learn"; the primary likewise has six lessons on "The Worth of One Person"; the junior topic is "Seeing Possibilities"; the high-school topic is "An American's Worth to Society"; and the seniors deal with "The Meaning of Life for Jesus." In the second year the general theme under "Sense of Worth" for a similar period is called "Experiences in Which People Find Their Best Selves"; and in the third year the general theme for the school is "Resources Equal to Growing Spiritual Needs." Each year there is a new approach, with new illustrations, to the same general type of religious experience. In using this functional approach, it will be readily understood that, though the focus of attention for a given period may be on "Sense of Worth," the situations used to make this meaningful are likely to involve one or more of the other nine types of religious experience. We do not try to isolate sense of worth, social sensitivity, or any of the other types of experience, but we do seek to identify these spiritual factors and to make them vital elements in appreciation of a religious way of living. Instead of leaving the impression of religion as a vague kind of goodness, we endeavor to give concrete and specific character to the ideas, attitudes, and adjustments involved in religious behavior. We also seek to make the three-year cycle, in the developmental program, as comprehensive as possible, so that a pupil going through a school using this functional curriculum would have a progressive and varied experience. In traditional programs the tendency has been to give a limited, general, repetitive set of experiences.

The following list of general themes used to date in this experimental curriculum suggests the wide range of situations which may be explored for religious meaning and evaluation. This list is supplemented immediately by illustrations as to how the departmental topics and lessons are developed in relation to the general theme.

GENERAL THEMES IN THREE-YEAR CYCLE OF THE
UNIFIED FUNCTIONAL CURRICULUM

I. THE BIBLE
A. The Bible's Contribution to Our Religion
B. People of the Bible Everyone Should Know
C. Bible Events To Be Remembered

II. SENSE OF WORTH
A. Spiritual Possibilities in Growing Lives
B. Experiences in Which People Find Their Best Selves
C. Resources Equal to Growing Spiritual Needs

III. SOCIAL SENSITIVITY
A. Christian Social Sensitivity
B. Knowing Our Fellow-Americans
C. Friendly Relations throughout the World

IV. DISCRIMINATION IN VALUES
A. Sacrificing for Higher Values
B. Discriminations: Unworthy Behavior, Worthy Acts, Ideals

C. The Price of Progress: Vision and Sacrifice

V. RESPONSIBILITY AND ACCOUNTABILITY
A. Responsibility in Christian Living
B. The Use of Freedom
C. Mutual Responsibilities and Modern Morals

VI. QUEST FOR TRUTH AND REALIZATION OF VALUES
A. The Christian Quest
B. Questers of the Centuries
C. Significant Quests

VII. CO-OPERATIVE FELLOWSHIP
A. The Church a Co-operative Fellowship
B. Organizations Which Further Christian Ideals
C. The Spirit of Religious Community Grows

VIII. APPRECIATION OF THE UNIVERSE
A. At Home in the Universe
B. Science and Religion
C. God and the Universe

The order which we have taken in presenting the units in a year's program is a compromise between psychological needs and the desire to take advantage of seasonal and special events of a year. We begin with the historical, giving lessons on the Bible. This is done for two reasons: (1) to make the transition to this type of curriculum easier for those accustomed to Bible emphasis in church-school teaching and (2) to give a biblical background for the many references to persons and incidents of the Bible which are bound to occur. Later other kinds of historical units may be added as electives or for other groups outside the church-school plan. The present arrangement of the other units was established when the units were first set up on a monthly basis, but, as these have been extended to six weeks, the sequence has not the same significance. It has proved fairly satisfactory to have such units as those on "Social Sensitivity" include the Christmas season; those on "Responsibility" deal with citizenship duties related to Lincoln's and Washington's birthdays; those on "Co-operative Fellowship" and the "Quest" come around Easter, when church membership and its obligations are emphasized; those on "Appreciation of the Universe" given in the spring, when nature is stimulating thoughts of creativity, beauty, and sustaining resources. The development of topics and lessons for each grade has been conditioned in this experiment by the necessity of using published materials to a large degree. Manuals, or guide sheets, have been prepared to adapt the existing publications to teaching situations under this functional approach. As it becomes possible to engage age-group specialists to write needed texts, there may be much greater freedom in selecting and editing lesson materials. Quite a large number of new units have been tentatively written where there were no available writings, and these are being enriched with widening experience and further studies.

No child under such a program of studies will have reason to say, as some do now in the high-school period, "We've had this same stuff ever since kindergarten." The units present subjects at each age level which are fresh, stimulating, and progressively complex, challenging attention and interest. It is hoped that they can be illustrated with pictures, projects, and reference materials, which are kept up to date and which give occasion for considering the ever changing situations of personal-social life. There are inexhaustible sources for enrichment of curricular studies based on this functional analytic study of religion.

The principle underlying our development of graded units is that the basic experiences grow with expanding knowledge and deepening insight and that quite different factors may affect growth at succeeding age levels. Though the general theme for the whole school may be the same for a six-weeks period, the lessons under departmental units will be distinctly different in content. The following outline of departmental units in the three-year cycle indicates our attempt to find topics under which suitable lessons can be selected for meeting age-group needs. Studies of children, youth, and adults, in varied situations, should be made continuously to keep lesson materials at a maximum of usefulness. Many of the topics now being used are unsatisfactory, but in this type of experiment one chooses the best that can be found or written and then revises, or replaces, the first forms by later improvements. We submit these imperfect forms merely as suggestive of needed lines of research and development.

GRADED UNITS IN THE THREE-YEAR CYCLE OF THE UNIFIED FUNCTIONAL CURRICULUM

I. The Bible

Kindergarten:
  A. The Bible in Pictures
  B. Family Pictures from the Bible
  C. Interesting Bible Writings

Primary:
  A. Jesus: The Baby, Boy, and Man
  B. Story People of the Bible
  C. Churches of Long Ago

Juniors:
  A. What Is in the Bible?
  B. Heroes of the Old Testament
  C. Bible Festivals

High School:
  A. Origin and Growth of the Bible
  B. Paul: Founder of the First Christian Churches
  C. Facts about Jesus Worth Knowing

Seniors:
  A. Different Values in the Bible
  B. Builders of the Hebrew Religion
  C. Backgrounds of the Old Testament

II. Sense of Worth

Kindergarten:
- A. Children Grow and Learn
- B. Finding Myself and Growing
- C. Things I Am Going To Do

Primary:
- A. The Worth of One Person
- B. A World with Plenty for Everyone
- C. Useful Living around the World

Juniors:
- A. Seeing Possibilities
- B. Better than Miracles

- C. How Rich Are We?

High School:
- A. An American's Worth to Society
- B. Experiences Which Stimulated Paul
- C. It Can Be Done

Seniors:
- A. The Meaning of Life for Jesus
- B. History Re-evaluates Hebrew Heroes
- C. Resources in Ourselves for Christian Living

III. Social Sensitivity

Kindergarten:
- A. Living Happily with Other People
- B. People Who Go Up and Down Our Street
- C. Other Countries: Other People

Primary:
- A. Children Who Need Better Opportunities
- B. Interesting Differences in People
- C. Finding Friends Everywhere

Juniors:
- A. China: Bright Sky Tomorrow

- B. Knowing Our Mexican Neighbors
- C. Getting Acquainted with Russians

High School:
- A. The Thrill of Seeing Others Make Good
- B. Can Americans Respect One Another?
- C. Friendly Relations around the World

Seniors:
- A. The Scapegoat
- B. Results of Americanization
- C. Christianity and a Better World

IV. Discrimination in Values

Kindergarten:
- A. Which Is Better?
- B. Wise and Foolish Ways of Living
- C. Planning Ahead

Primary:
- A. Two Kinds of Selves
- B. Good Examples and Not So Good
- C. Fun in Doing Hard Things

Juniors:
A. Price of Peace and Good Will
B. Mexicans Seek Larger Opportunities
C. What Did War Teach Us?

High School:
A. Making Life Count
B. Compare, If You Will?

C. Overcoming Prejudices That Block Progress

Seniors:
A. Competing Programs for World Order
B. Changing Customs and Standards
C. Progressive Achievements in Living

V. RESPONSIBILITY AND ACCOUNTABILITY

Kindergarten:
A. Learning Self-management
B. Big Enough To Be Trusted
C. Understanding Why

Primary:
A. Thinking Before Acting
B. Made To, or Free To
C. Rules for Both Sides

Juniors:
A. The Wise Use of Money
B. Christian Democratic Freedom

C. Who Is Responsible?

High School:
A. A Good Citizen
B. Americans Who Appreciate Freedom
C. Responsibilities in Majorities

Seniors:
A. Democratic Ideals
B. Religion, Ethics, and Freedom
C. Mutual Responsibilities in Personal Friendships

VI. THE QUEST

Kindergarten:
A. Interesting Things To Investigate
B. Discovering Secrets
C. Worth Doing

Primary:
A. Finding Rules To Live By
B. Questions Boys and Girls Ask
C. What We Need and Want

Juniors:
A. The Quest for Peace
B. Artists Who Discovered the Beautiful

C. Inventions Requiring Wise Control

High School:
A. What Is "God's Will"?
B. Founders of Christian Movements
C. Life Investment

Seniors:
A. Quest for the Good Life
B. Founders of Non-Christian Religions
C. Religious Leaders of the Last Century

VII. Co-operative Fellowship

Kindergarten:
A. Living Happily with Other People
B. Organizations Which Help To Make a Good City
C. How Animals Work Together

Primary:
A. Leaders in Our Church
B. Working Together in Christian Ways
C. Widening Ways of Co-operation

Juniors:
A. Our Church and Other Churches
B. Organizations Which Make Ideas

C. Churches at Work in the Community

High School:
A. Privileges and Responsibilities of Church Membership
B. Youth Organizations in America
C. Spirit of Community Living

Seniors:
A. Understanding Other Denominations
B. Organizations for Social Betterment
C. Social Creeds and Social Action

VIII. Appreciation of the Universe

Kindergarten:
A. The World We Live In
B. We Wonder
C. Enjoying New Things Every Day

Primary:
A. Beauty and Wonder in Out-of-Doors
B. Learning Nature's Secrets
C. What Makes Life Good?

Juniors:
A. Ancient and Modern Stories of Creation
B. Ways That Stimulate Thought and Worship

C. Different Ideas of God

High School:
A. Your World and How To Live in It
B. Science and Religion Tackle Alcohol
C. Meanings of Familiar Hymns

Seniors:
A. Prayer in a World of Science
B. The Bible and Science
C. Biblical Ideas of God and the Universe

In addition to the vertical sequence of units, we have tried in a few cases to provide for a horizontal development; for some find interest sustained well through two related units. It may be possible to make pairs of all, with two phases of a common set of interests. This was done in Units I and II of the second-year sequence of the junior, high-school, and senior lessons. Thus, the unit for juniors on "Heroes of the Old Testament" was followed by one called "Better than Miracles," in which each of the Old Testament heroes was paralleled by a modern character who performed as great acts as the Ancients, without any miracle story attached to his achievements. The study of "Paul: Founder of the First Christian Churches" continued with a psychological examination of Paul's experiences and sense of worth, in a unit entitled "Experiences Which Stimulated Paul." And in the senior department, "Builders of the Hebrew Religion" led to a re-examination of the records in the unit, "History Re-evaluates Hebrew Heroes." Several other combinations of this kind were tried, all with interesting results. In two or three cases we worked six weeks on a topic, left it for another unit, and came back on new phases of the general area in a new topic.

Though six weeks seems a short time for developing any basic experience, it must be kept in mind that in this functional approach we have complex life-situations in every lesson, with many opportunities for giving attention to some factor involved in our ten categories. Without repeatedly speaking of sense of worth, social sensitivity, or any of the other general qualities, a teacher may cause pupils to face the alternatives of worthy and unworthy behavior and to recognize different degrees of religious sensitivity in personal-social adjustments. The six-weeks unit does give occasion for an intensive study in one special field of interest and provides about the right length of unit for leadership training. Teachers may be helped to think through objectives and methods for a short unit and to feel some sense of confidence in handling a group in such a limited type of study. This experiment has kept in mind constantly the limitations of the rank and file of teachers who may be expected to use these lessons in the ordinary church school. Even younger pupils can sense the meaning and hold objectives in mind for a short unit; and if it is rich in stimulating material, there is a better chance of regular attendance and pupil participation than when a unit is extended over months with its aims vague and its continuity of meaning difficult to appreciate. It is much better for children to want more study on a topic than to feel bored by keeping at one too long. The experiences of life are disjunctive, though they do have various connecting interests, and it is more a matter of methods in teaching than subject matter whether children feel relatedness in the sequence of lessons. The short units help to keep specific factors clear, give occasions for dealing with many concrete situations of varied character, and invite frequent reviews of progress in thinking. There are many ways of weaving them together into a unified pattern of religious living, through worship, dramatizations, school papers, and other projects. The main need is for the teachers to feel that this ten-point analysis is but a means of identifying and interpreting the component factors in a total life-process.

A sample list of lessons in one set of units for a six-weeks period will illustrate how every Sunday may have an abundance of fresh and stimulating experiences for all grades. A teacher of average ability can add many personal experiences and draw from the class others to enrich the meanings and appreciations of any lesson. In a workers' conference before the unit begins, resources may be reviewed and methods of work may be demonstrated, so that confidence and skills may be wisely developed. The following titles will suggest many possibilities to any reader.

VII. CO-OPERATIVE FELLOWSHIP

SECOND YEAR: ORGANIZATIONS WHICH FURTHER CHRISTIAN IDEALS

Kindergarten: Organizations Which Make a Good City
1. Homes are the most important places
2. We need doctors and hospitals for sick people
3. Playgrounds and parks are good places to have fun
4. School teaches us to think and to know many things
5. Stores enable us to buy what we need
6. Churches are special places to go on Sundays

Primary: Working Together in Christian Ways
1. What makes a home Christian?
2. Doing things together in springtime
3. Christian ways of doing business in our stores

4. What school teaches about Christian ways
5. The Christian spirit in hospitals and relief work
6. Keeping the Christian spirit active in our churches

Juniors: Organizations Which Make Ideas
1. Ideas may start in discussion groups
2. Current papers and periodicals give up-to-date ideas
3. Books worth reading
4. What the radio gives us to think about
5. The kind of movies worth seeing
6. Church groups analyze all ideas

High school: Youth Organizations in America
1. Scouting in America
2. 4-H clubs in rural America
3. Junior Red Cross
4. Y.M.C.A. and Y.W.C.A.— boys' and girls' programs
5. Boys Brotherhood Republic
6. Denominational youth organizations

Seniors: Organizations for Social Betterment
1. Social service agencies
2. Educational and social-reform agencies
3. Co-operative movements and interracial organizations
4. Peace movements and international organizations
5. Recreational agencies
6. Social-action committees in the churches

Helps for leaders and teachers are provided in reference books, sample worship services, and a manual of suggestions for each Sunday's program. Considerable initiative is expected by both the departmental leader and the class teacher, and freedom is permitted in adapting lessons to pupil needs and interests. The outline of one Sunday's program for a junior group will illustrate the kind of helps which have been provided to date. In a few units we have developed workbooks for pupils, but a great deal remains to be done in assembling resource materials for leaders and teachers and for project work by pupils. We need stories, pictures, films, sample work projects, dramatizations, correlations with public school activities and studies, hymns, ritual, and many other suggestive ideas and methods of work at all age levels.

LESSON GUIDE

Theme for Church School: Organizations Which Further Christian Ideals

JUNIOR UNIT VII: ORGANIZATIONS WHICH MAKE IDEAS

Lesson 1.—Ideas may start in discussion groups.

General aim.—To help boys and girls to appreciate the many agencies of modern society which are influencing people's ideas of right and wrong, to cause them to discriminate, and to help further those ideas which are good and constructive.

Preparation.—This series of lessons comes under the type of experience which we have called "Co-operative Fellowship." Last year Unit VII dealt with the church, and we studied "Our Church and Other Churches." This year we look at what other organizations are doing to advance Christian ideas and values. If the church is effective, it must influence homes, schools, and other agencies of our communities; so that religion becomes a seven-day-a-week experience. Preview the six lessons and invite the pupils to bring in illustrative materials such as news items, school or play incidents, pictures, and problem situations.

Aim for Lesson 1.—To recall the many kinds of discussion groups in which juniors take part—family, friends, play groups, school classes, church, and special meetings; to think over examples of ways in which ideas are shaped and changed; to consider religion as a way of refining ideas and ideals to promote the best kind of living for individuals and for society.

Assembly presentation.—The leader may start with such questions as these, stimulating children to talk over their experiences: What is a discussion? Can you tell me of some discussions you have had this week? What starts a discussion? What is a good discussion? Are any rules needed for carrying on a good discussion among a number of people? What kinds of discussions do older people have? Do we have discussions about the things in which you are interested? Are there questions you might discuss in church which you would not be likely to discuss in school?

Note the value of talking things over, of getting other people's points of view; and of learning to listen respectfully to what others say. Pick out a number of illustrations from the Bible of discussions over problems of right and wrong, reasons for suffering, ideas of God, the most important things to do, etc. In the Old Testament in the Book of Job is a story of a long discussion of a man and his friends over many questions. In the New Testament Jesus was asked questions, and people would sit around and talk. The only picture of Jesus as a boy is one in which he came to the temple with his parents and found some priests who were interested in talking with him. Take two or three illustrations of discussions: Prayer (Matt. 6:5 ff., Luke 11:1 ff.). What is the Great Commandment? (Matt. 22:36 ff., Luke 10:25 ff.). Who is greatest? (Luke 9:46 ff., Mark 10:35 ff., John 13:1–15). What is God like? (Acts 17:22 ff., I John 4:7 ff.).

Let these youngsters feel that in religion we may think together, recall what other people have said in the Bible or in other places, and yet have many problems for which we cannot get final answers. Discussions may help us to think better and to get good working ideas which may grow as our knowledge grows. Note how people speak of ways which seem good for all as God's ways. Religion seeks these best-for-all ways of living.

Class session.—Discover how many listen in on radio discussions, such as the town meeting, interviews, quizzes, etc. See how frequently pupils work on school committees or have class discussions. Do they talk over problems which come up in school or on the playground?

Consider ways of making the church-school class discussions profitable. Think ahead, and have the class consider information which they might bring on the next topic to make discussion interesting and profitable. Recall the kind of goals we must keep in mind in discussions we shall call religious, goals that work toward universal principles, that are just and good for all. To be Christian we shall recall teachings of Jesus or standards which have grown up among Christian people. Note how the Golden Rule is one of these general principles.

Have a secretary keep records each Sunday, and distribute the responsibility, expecting all to do a good job in turn. Plan for a summary at end of unit.

Several weeks before a unit is to begin a workers' conference is held, with a preview of the lessons for each department and opportunities for each teacher and leader to get clear understanding of ends to be sought, materials available, creative work expected, and help on specific items as needed. Where dual leadership can be planned, one person takes major charge in one unit and another in the following unit. Two people working together stimulate and reinforce each other along lines that neither would be willing to undertake alone. In these conferences ministers and others are present as resource people, and, frequently, specialists from public schools or from the community are invited to share in planning and to take part in particular projects. The minister of the church is expected to launch each new set of units in the regular Sunday morning church service, on the Sundays preceding the beginning of the units. Thus before the units on "Sense of Worth" the minister may speak of this type of experience as central in religion, give illustrations of the values of lessons in this area for all ages, and suggest how homes and other community agencies may further the ends sought. This makes the church school an integral part of the church program instead of a layman's annex. The minister may set a keynote and create a needed interest and support for the church school.

In a number of situations parents have asked for special classes to help them make this functional religion more effective in their homes. Typical home situations may be analyzed, and parents may exchange experiences. In co-operative thinking not only will individuals find help and develop better skills in home affairs but community problems may be dealt with and general environing conditions improved. In one case a public school principal was especially helpful for a group of parents, for she was able to give many illustrations of ways in which both home and school could work on the same goals suggested by this set of basic religious experiences and supplement each other. In such ways religion is removed from its ordinary vague, sentimental exhortations and given specific concrete meaning in ordinary everyday adjustments of human living.

Some have asked whether this type of material could be used in weekday religious education on released public school time. Undoubtedly, this functional curriculum is less sectarian than most materials and could be readily integrated into the total educational experience, but there is a question whether the sectarian leaders most likely to sponsor a weekday program would be willing to use this critical, creative approach. Most religious leaders are accustomed to think of religious education as a matter of uncritical indoctrination without examination of presuppositions in prayers, theological references, hymns, rituals, and general teachings. Instead of trying to add religion to general education by a scheme of teaching lessons of either the traditional kind or this functional type, it would seem wiser to define religion in functional terms and to identify its pervasive qualities. Spiritual ends should be sought in every part of general education, not in a once-a-week addendum of an hour's special service. Until churchmen are willing to permit free discussion of conflicting views and to encourage critical-historical study of religious ideas and practices, it will be impossible to deal satisfactorily with controversial theological views and ecclesiastical customs, but it might be practical to unite on some phases of this functional analysis of religion. Gradually, people may recognize that religion must transcend sectarianism and be freed from its uncritical forms, and the spirit of religion at its best will pervade the common life.

The primary purpose of this experiment and of this report is to encourage a functional approach to religious education; to indicate how this may be done at all age levels; to suggest how it makes available a rich and stimulating body of source materials which make religion most vital for current living; to make clear that the controversial questions which divide religious people may be frankly and effectively dealt with when indoctrination gives place to creative educational procedures. The achievements are imperfect, but the lines of further fruitful study and co-operative action are made clear.

Notes and References

CHAPTER ONE

1. For critical-historical studies of religion showing its developmental character:

    E. S. AMES. *Religion.* New York: Henry Holt & Co., 1929.

    A. E. HAYDON. *The Quest of the Ages.* New York: Harper & Bros., 1929.
    Man's Search for the Good Life. New York: Harper & Bros., 1937.
    A Biography of the Gods. New York: Macmillan Co., 1941.

    S. J. CASE. *Jesus through the Centuries.* Chicago: University of Chicago Press, 1932.
    Christianity in a Changing World. New York: Harper & Bros., 1941.

2. For interpretation of naturalism:

    H. N. WIEMAN and B. MELAND. *American Philosophies of Religion.* Chicago: Willett, Clark & Co., 1936.

    E. A. BURTT. *Types of Religious Philosophy.* New York: Harper & Bros., 1939.

    Y. H. KRIKORIAN *et al. Naturalism and the Human Spirit.* New York: Columbia University Press, 1944.

    H. H. DUBS. "Religious Naturalism, an Evaluation," *Journal of Religion,* XXIII (October, 1943), 258–65.

    W. C. BOWER. "Points of Tension between Progressive Religious Education and Current Theological Trends," *Religious Education,* XXXIV (April–June and July–September, 1939), 69–72, 164–81.

3. For critical studies of the concept of God:

    S. MATHEWS. *The Growth of the Idea of God.* New York: Macmillan Co., 1931.
    Is God Emeritus? New York: Macmillan Co., 1940.

    E. S. AMES. "New Trends in Thinking about God," *Journal of Religion,* XXI (October, 1941), 373–84.

    W. H. BERNHARDT. "An Analytic Approach to the God Concept," *Religion in the Making,* II (March, 1942), 252 ff.
    "The Cognitive Quest for God," *Journal of Religion,* XXIII (April, 1943), 91–102.

    H. N. WIEMAN. "Can God Be Perceived?" *Journal of Religion,* XXIII (January, 1943), 23–32.

4. For a study of the Bible in the light of social experiences:

    W. C. BOWER. *The Living Bible.* New York: Harper & Bros., 1936.

CHAPTER TWO

1. The functional point of view in religion is well expressed by:
   W. C. BOWER. *Christ and Christian Education*, chap. ii. Nashville: Abingdon-Cokesbury Press, 1943.
   Faith of the Free, chap. i (ed. W. E. GARRISON). Chicago: Willett, Clark & Co., 1940.
   H. S. ELLIOTT. *Can Religious Education Be Christian?* New York: Macmillan Co., 1940.

2. For other uses of the functional point of view in modern education:
   J. DEWEY and J. L. CHILDS. "Implications of the Idea of Education as a Social Operation," *Progressive Education*, XV (March, 1938), 244–45.
   EDUCATIONAL POLICIES COMMISSION. *The Unique Function of Education in American Democracy.* Washington: National Education Association, 1937.
   The Purposes of Education in American Democracy. Washington: National Education Association, 1938.
   I. B. BERKSON. *Education Faces the Future.* New York: Harper & Bros., 1943.

3. A good illustration of the spiritual emphasis in education is:
   J. S. BRUBACHER *et al.* "The Public Schools and Spiritual Values," in *Seventh Yearbook of the John Dewey Society.* New York: Harper & Bros., 1944.

4. See GEORGE A. COE's frequent reference to this major objective:
   Social Theory of Religious Education. New York: Charles Scribner's Sons, 1917.
   What Is Christian Education? New York: Charles Scribner's Sons, 1929. (Note especially chap. iv, "The Creative Principle of the Worth of Persons.")

CHAPTER THREE

1. For further illustrations of educational emphasis on development of sense of worth and social sensitivity:
   K. W. BIGELOW *et al. Teachers for Our Times.* (Note end points of personality development.) Washington: American Council on Education, 1944.
   C. M. MACCONNELL, E. O. MELBY, and C. O. ARNDT. *New Schools for a New Culture.* New York: Harper & Bros., 1944.
   EDUCATIONAL POLICIES COMMISSION. *Purposes of Education in American Democracy.* (Note the two primary objectives, self-realization and human relationships, chaps. iv and v.) Washington: Progressive Education Association, 1938.
   COMMITTEE ON THE RELATION OF SCHOOL AND COLLEGE. *Thirty Schools Tell Their Story.* (Vol. V in *Adventures in American Education.*) (Note Denver's core-curriculum joining objectives in personal living with personal-social relationships and social community relationship.) New York: Harper & Bros., 1943.
   F. T. SPAULDING. *High School and Life.* (Regent's inquiry of the University of the State of New York. Need for social conscience and social responsibility.) New York: McGraw-Hill Book Co., Inc., 1938.

CHAPTER FOUR

1. Compare the teachings of any church-school quarterly or those of such books as:
   M. A. Jones. *Tell Me about God*. Chicago: Rand, McNally & Co., 1943.
   F. M. Fitch. *One God: The Ways We Worship Him*. New York: Lothrop, Lee & Shephard Co., 1944.
   R. Trent. *Your Child and God*. Chicago: Willett, Clark & Co., 1941.
   with the nonindoctrinating naturalistic presentations of:
   B. Stevens. *Child and the Universe*. New York: John Day & Co., 1931.
         How Miracles Abound. New York: John Day & Co., 1941.
   S. L. Fahs. *Beginnings of Earth and Sky*. Boston: Beacon Press, 1938.
   M. M. and F. Eakin. *Your Child's Religion*. New York: Macmillan Co., 1942.

2. For illustrations of children's confusion from theological indoctrination and irrational use of the term God:
   L. J. Sherrill. *The Opening Doors of Childhood*. New York: Macmillan Co., 1939.
   A. Munkres. *Which Way for Our Children?* New York: Charles Scribner's Sons, 1936.

3. For a discussion of growth in moral discrimination see chap. ix in the author's book, *Personality Development in Children* (Chicago: University of Chicago Press, 1937).

4. For problems of discipline in school situations and ways of developing self-controlled personalities with sense of social responsibilities:
   G. V. Sheviakov and F. Redl, *Discipline for Today's Children and Youth*. Washington: National Education Association, 1944.

CHAPTER FIVE

1. For methods of developing responsibility as citizens and effective members of a democracy see such books as:
   Educational Policies Commission. *Learning the Ways of Democracy*. Washington: National Education Association, 1940.
   George S. Counts. *The Schools Can Teach Democracy*. New York: John Day Co., 1939.
   M. Curti. *Social Ideals of American Educators*. New York: Charles Scribner's Sons, 1935.

2. R. W. Gerard. "Higher Levels of Integration," *Science*, XCV (March 27, 1942), 309–13. (Quotation is from address given at Fiftieth Anniversary of University of Chicago, on which article is based.)

3. Department of Supervisors and Directors of Instruction. *Eleventh Yearbook*, "Cooperation: Principles and Practices." Washington: National Education Association, 1939.

4. B. Goodykoontz and B. Coon. *Family Living and Our Schools*. (Note how school studies in family living are directed toward larger democratic responsibilities.) New York: Appleton-Century Co., 1941.

5. For illustrations of studies in group experience:

J. L. MORENO. *Who Shall Survive?* Washington: Nervous and Mental Disease Publishing Co., 1934.

G. COYLE. *Studies in Group Behavior.* New York: Harper & Bros., 1937.

H. S. DIMOCK. *Rediscovering the Adolescent.* New York: Association Press, 1937.

B. and R. CASSIDY. *Group Experience, the Democratic Way.* New York: Harper & Bros., 1943.

6. E. L. THORNDIKE. *Man and His Works,* chap iii. Cambridge: Harvard University Press, 1943. (Note how the author emphasizes the fact that "cooperativeness is multifarious and specialized," resembling a merchant's stock of goods. This spiritual quality, as also the other nine of our basic religious experiences, shows a growing ability to profit by the stimulation of widening relationship and developing cultures.)

CHAPTER SIX

1. H. R. ANDERSON. "Teaching Critical Thinking in Our Social Studies," *Thirteenth Yearbook of the National Council for the Social Studies.* Washington: National Education Association, 1942.

2. G. A. COE. *Educating for Citizenship,* chap. iv. New York: Charles Scribner's Sons, 1934.

W. C. BOWER. *Character through Creative Experience.* Chicago: University of Chicago Press, 1930.

3. INTERNATIONAL COUNCIL OF RELIGIOUS EDUCATION. *Curriculum Guide,* Book I: *Objectives in Religious Education.* Chicago: International Council of Religious Education, 1932.

4. For illustrations of questions which children frequently ask and examples of ways in which they are answered:

M. BRO. *When Children Ask.* Chicago: Willett, Clark & Co., 1940.

A. MUNKRES. *Which Way for Our Children?* New York: Charles Scribner's Sons, 1936.

L. J. SHERRILL. *The Opening Doors of Childhood.* New York: Macmillan Co., 1939.

5. L. T. HOPKINS *et al. Integration, Its Meaning and Applications.* New York: Appleton-Century, 1937.

6. H. HARTSHORNE and M. MAY. *Studies in Deceit.* New York: Macmillan Co., 1928. (Note especially evaluation of hortative methods of conditioning conduct, p. 413.)

7. For educational trends in integrating community influences:

EDUCATIONAL POLICIES COMMISSION. *Education for All American Youth.* Washington: National Education Association, 1944.

R. S. LYND. *Knowledge for What?* Princeton: Princeton University Press, 1939.

R. LINTON. *The Cultural Backgrounds of Personality.* Washington: American Council on Education, 1941.

8. For analysis of issues in weekday religious education and released public school time:
C. H. MOEHLMAN. *School and Church: The American Way*. New York: Harper & Bros., 1944.
W. C. BOWER. *Church and State in Education*. Chicago: University of Chicago Press, 1944.
Weekday Religious Education. Bulletin No. 3. Washington: U.S. Office of Education, 1941.

CHAPTER SEVEN

1. LORD VANSITTART. "Germany's Third Try," *Atlantic Monthly*, CLXXVI (August, 1945), 43.
2. For discussions on interpretation and use of the Bible, see such books as:
W. C. BOWER. *The Living Bible*. New York: Harper & Bros,, 1936.
G. CHAMBERLAIN. *Making the Bible Live*. Chicago: University of Chicago Press, 1939.
T. G. SOARES. *The Origins of the Bible*. New York: Harper & Bros., 1941.
L. WALLIS. *The Bible Is Human*. New York: Columbia University Press, 1942.
3. R. DUBOIS. *Get Together Americans*. New York: Harper & Bros., 1943. (This is a good illustration of the use of community festivals.)

CHAPTER EIGHT

1. W. C. BOWER. "Religious Education Faces the Future," *Journal of Religion*, XXI October, 1941), 385–97. (Note also recent issues of *Religious Education,* an interfaith journal of the Religious Education Association, given primarily to front-line problems.)
2. For suggestive methods and techniques in general education and for examples of attempts to bridge the gap between the two processes of general and religious education see such books as:
S. G. COLE. *Character and Christian Education*. Nashville: Cokesbury Press, 1936.
DEPARTMENT OF SUPERVISION AND CURRICULUM DEVELOPMENT. *Toward a New Curriculum*. Washington: National Education Association, 1944.
J. S. BRUBACHER *et al. The Public School and Spiritual Values*. New York: Harper & Bros., 1944.

Index

Adolescents, 17, 42–43, 47–48, 65; group influence on, 71–72, 84–85, 86, 106

Appreciation: of historical continuity, 31, 110–18, 129, 134; of the universe, 24, 55–65, 132, 154

Atomic bomb, 2, 126, 142, 145

Bible, the, 7, 10, 31, 112–13, 129, 136, 149; curriculum units in, 151

Church, 8, 28, 32, 49, 85, 90, 107, 124, 129

Conscience, 78, 103

Co-operative fellowship, 27–28, 81–90, 133, 154, 156–58

Critical creative thinking, vi, 2, 12, 30, 68, 80, 94, 98, 102, 109–10, 116, 126, 134–36

Curriculum, vii, 31, 143, 146–61

Democracy, 94, 141

Discipline, 77

Discrimination in values, 26, 65–72, 132, 152–53

Divine, the, viii, 8, 36, 54

Dualism, 6, 94, 131

Education, 19, 41, 77, 92; *see also* Public-school influences

Emotions, 29, 140

Family, 32, 48, 83–84, 123, 138, 160

Functional religion, 14–15, 17–34, 35, 90, 110, 115, 131, 139

George Davis Bivin Foundation, vii

Gerard, R. W., 82

God, 10, 24–25, 54, 59, 62–63, 78, 96, 112, 119

Group celebrations; *see* Participation in group celebrations

Hebraic-Christian traditions, 1, 56, 96, 116, 142

Indoctrination, 3, 13, 44, 56, 94–96, 111–12, 117, 135

Integration of experiences, 29, 33–34, 99–107, 134

International Council of Religious Education, objectives of, 95

Jesus, 3, 11, 14–15, 30–31, 66, 103

Kingdom of God, 27–28, 81

Labor unions, 87–88, 101

Leadership, 39–40, 155, 159

Mental measurement, 18–19

Motivation, 22, 68–69

Myrdal, Dr. Gunnar, 50

Naturalism, vi, 6–7, 13, 23, 57, 97, 114, 120, 128, 130, 137

Participation in group celebrations, 32–33, 118, 134–35

Plural possibilities, world of, 131, 145

Prayer, 27, 58, 63, 122, 130–31

Public-school influences, 34, 38, 46–47, 48, 59–60, 75, 85, 92, 93, 123; nursery school, 38, 61, 75; first grade, 46, 75; second grade, 59; third grade, 39–40; fourth grade, 47; fifth grade, 40, 60;